June 14, 1993

KENOSIS

Dear Kathy, Jim, Greg & Doug.
  It's been a pleasure celebrating life & the faith with you. I know where you live... so!
  I hope Jesus touches your heart in some way as you read through this part of my journey of Kenosis & as your own adventure continues to unfold. I'll miss you.
  All the best always.
It's been fun!

love
f. Kev, ofm

KENOSIS

*Emptying Self and the
Path of Christian Service*

KEVIN M. CRONIN, O.F.M.

ELEMENT

Rockport, Massachusetts ● Shaftesbury, Dorset

© 1992 Kevin M. Cronin

Published in the U.S.A. in 1992 by
Element, Inc.
42 Broadway, Rockport, MA 01966

Published in Great Britain in 1992 by
Element Books Limited
Longmead, Shaftesbury, Dorset

Cover illustration *St Francis* by *Berlinghieri*
Courtesy of Scala
Cover design by Barbara McGavin
Text design by Roger Lightfoot
Typeset by Colset Pte Ltd, Singapore
Printed in the United States of America by
Edwards Brothers, Inc

Library of Congress Cataloging-in-Publication Data
Cronin, Kevin.
Kenosis : emptying self and the path of Christian service
Kevin Cronin.
Includes bibliographical references.
1. Christian life—Catholic authors.   2. Self-denial.   3. Service
(Theology)   4. Church work with the poor—New York (N.Y.)
5. Cronin, Kevin.   I. Title.
BX2350.2.C72   1992   248.4'82—dc20   91–26160

British Library Cataloguing in Publication Data available

ISBN 1–85230–285–2

DEDICATION

I dedicate this work to:

The memory of my beloved parents, Annette and John Cronin. Mom taught me to dance, to be compassionate, to cherish and to celebrate life! Dad gave me self-discipline, inner strength, confidence, and courage!

To the wonderful teachers with whom I've been blessed:

Dr. Carol Bandini Mamorella; Fr. Edward W. Troike; Sisters of St. Dominic, Amityville, NY; American Martyrs School, Bayside; Theophane Larkin, OFM; Brennan Connelly, OFM; Elmer Wagner, OFM; Eric Kyle, OFM; Rene Willet; Daniel O'Rourke; Dr. Roy Bodie; George McLean OMI; Edmund Dobbin OSA; Damien McElrath; Cassian Corcoran, OFM; Michael Scanlon, OSA; Shaun McCarty, ST; Vincent Cushing, OFM; Regis Duffy, OFM.

Never act out of rivalry or conceit; rather let all parties think humbly of others as superior to themselves, each of you looking to others' interests rather than your own (Phil. 2:3).

Your attitude must be that of Christ:

> Though he was in the form of God,
> he did not deem equality to God
> something to be grasped at.
>
> Rather, he *emptied himself (Kenosis)*
> and took the form of a slave
> being born in the likeness of men and women.
>
> He was known to be of human estate,
> and it was thus that he humbled himself,
> obediently accepting even death,
> death on a cross.
>
> Because of this God highly exalted him and bestowed
> on him the name above every other name,
> So that at Jesus' name
> every knee must bend
> in the heavens, on the earth, and
> under the earth, and every tongue proclaim
> to the Glory of God the Father.
> *Jesus Christ is Lord!* (*Phil.* 2:6–11)

Contents

Acknowledgments

I would like first to give praise to the Life-Giver and Creator of all people, who calls me into life with Jesus Christ and community in the Order of Friars Minor.

I would like to cite some of those Friars Minor for their competent assistance and brotherly support: Blaise Hamaday, O.F.M., who was my supervisor and reflected with me throughout the experience, and who gave me many valuable insights into both myself and the ministry; Emeric Meier, O.F.M., who guided me throughout the initial writing of this manuscript. His patience and availability were greatly appreciated.

The friars at St. Francis of Assisi Church in New York City are to be acknowledged for their hospitality and their willingness to allow me to serve with them as a member of their community.

A special word of thanks goes to my sister, Annette Veronica Kopp, who typed my second draft, and who encouraged me when the going got rough. Also to Mary Ellen Leibla who put the manuscript on computer for me.

And of course, the people of New York City are to be acknowledged, the small and the great alike, who allowed me to serve them, who received much from me, but gave me much more than they could ever imagine!

A very special word of joyful thanks goes to Naomi Gilpatrick who discovered this work sixteen years after it was written. By God's grace and mysterious workings, with her help, it will now be shared with a greater public.

Introduction: Why Kenosis?

Kenosis is at the heart of Christian life as well as at the core of ministry. Kenosis is a resolute divesting of the person of every claim of self-interest so as to be ready to live the Gospel of Christ in every aspect of living, freed from the dictates of personal preference. Jesus said to all:

> If anyone wishes to come after me, he must deny himself and take up his cross daily and follow me. For whoever wishes to save his life will lose it, but whoever loses his life for my sake will save it (*Luke* 9: 23).

You will ask: How can I enact out Kenosis in my life? How can I go about denying my very self at every turn?

To show you how a modern man of twenty-five in the heart of a busy modern city, New York, resolved to express Kenosis in action, I kept a journal of whom I met and what each encounter cost me when I attempted selfless giving. It was an adventure of the spirit. From my experiences with God, with myself, with strangers, with the Franciscan friars with whom I share the drive to serve, you may get intimations of how you, too, can enter into this great adventure of denying self.

Getting at the heart of things has always been an admirable trait of the followers of Francis of Assisi. St. Francis himself spoke "plainly and simply." He also lived that way. Unencumbered by distractions, he lived life from the inside out, from the core of his being. At that core was the person of Christ Jesus and the mystery of his love.

I was fortunate to come into contact with the Friars Minor at the age of fourteen. Seeking to become a Franciscan priest, I entered their high school seminary in Callicoon, New York in 1962. In many ways I grew up with them, the last of a dying breed of high school seminarians.

I know that through osmosis I picked up some of that spirit which gets right to the heart of the matter, displayed by so many different friars I encountered at St. Joe's.

I believe, however, that I was previously disposed to this characteristic even before I met them. As a child of eleven, I experienced the tragic mystery of "sister death" at the loss of my beloved mother. Even at such an early age, this emptiness caused me to think about what really is most important in life. I think I grew up a little faster than some of my peers.

All through my studies and exposure to St. Francis, I often tried to understand questions such as: What made him tick? What's behind this poverty deal? Why this love of nature?

It made me wonder about Jesus Christ also. What is at his core? Is there one prism through which we can view him? Is there one prism through which I can view me?

Entertaining questions such as these, I looked at my prism, which had often been Francis, and I came upon Kenosis. Francis was fascinated with the Kenosis of Jesus Christ, from the "emptying of his divinity, taking on the nature of a slave" at the first Christmas in Bethlehem, to the final divesting of it on the cross on Calvary, "accepting even death, death on a cross."

Francis was consumed by the mysterious love of God who chose to become poor that we might become rich. As we hear in the Liturgy at the mingling of the water with the wine: "May we come to share in the divinity of Christ who humbled himself to share in our humanity."

This humbling, this emptying, this letting go was something Francis longed for in imitation of his love, Jesus Christ. From the crib to the cross, I believe, the theme of Kenosis was at the very heart of God in Christ, and was the theme that ran through the pages of the Gospels from Bethlehem to Nazareth, from Galilee to Jerusalem.

From his experiences in Greccio and La Verna, Francis marveled at this love and wanted it for himself. He would say to himself in the words of St. Paul:

> I wish to know Christ and the power flowing from his resurrection; likewise how to share in his sufferings by being formed into the pattern of his death (*Phil.* 3: 10).

Francis wanted to be transformed through that same emptying, that same Kenosis, in imitation of the Christ he so loved. So much so, that towards the later part of his life, he plainly prayed for just that:

> My Lord Jesus Christ, I pray You to grant me two graces before I die: the first is that during my life I may feel in my soul and in my body, as much as possible, that pain which You, dear Jesus, sustained in the hour of Your most bitter passion. The second is that I may feel in my heart, as much as possible, that excessive love which You, O Son of God, were inflamed in willingly enduring such suffering for us sinners.[1]

History tells us that on Mt. La Verna his prayer was answered as Francis was transformed into a living image of the one he loved, bearing the sacred marks of the crucified, totally emptied Savior, who said the night before he died: "This is my body, given up for you." Used up totally! Words Jesus had lived his whole life long, only culminating in the actual crucifixion. Body given up, blood poured out. Nothing left. And in that total self-surrender, that one act of perfect love, one of our race redeemed us. One human acted like God, loving totally, and made all of us acceptable, restoring us into God's image. That Lamb of God took away the sins of the world. And on that cross we no longer saw the love of a man, but for one perfect moment that changed history, the human race saw the love of God made flesh. And in that revelation, we were promised that we, too, could reveal that Divine Love in our human love. And in being more human, we are really becoming more divine.

It is in the image of this God of Love that we were made. And it is when we love that we prove we know God, and we become more like Him. Kenosis is about love! It's about self-giving for the sake of others.

I'm just so surprised that it has never been written about under this name and title. I feel that it is the very core of Jesus, Francis, and anyone who wishes to follow them. In my studies at the Catholic University of America and at the Washington Theological Union, I could find no work to research with the title of Kenosis. Something so central and essential to both human love and Christian life had to be written about, displayed so that others may perhaps find what I had found.

Knowing about Kenosis is one matter. Doing it is another. That is one of the great things about this book. I talk about how I do it.

And I speak about how I don't do it, what keeps me from Kenosis, and living this vision of life.

I talk about four basic movements of Kenosis in my four chapters. I discuss each one and then evaluate myself and my ability to love and be kenotic. Where are my resistance spots? How do these affect the way I love and serve others? I know something about Kenosis, but I don't always do it. This book is an exploration of that vision of life I call Kenosis. St. Francis used to say that a "friar only truly knew what he could put into practice." You will see what I know about Kenosis, how I live up to it as a guiding theme in my life and ministry, and how I don't.

I hope that this theme can be useful to the reader in exploring your own life through the prism of Kenosis. This is only one man's scratching the surface of the mystery of human life. I hope that it is useful to others on their journey.

Last Thursday I saw a poster in a Christian bookstore that read "The main thing is to keep the main thing the main thing!" I liked it and I agree with it.

I believe Kenosis is the main thing! It's the secret nature continually reveals every spring after winter; in rainbows after the rain; in butterflies after cocoons. Easter Sunday after Good Friday in church terms. New life after dying to self. In the Peace prayer: "It is in dying that we are born!"

Most of us, myself included, would much prefer to live outside the open tomb on Easter Sunday and skip right past Mt. Calvary! But I believe that there is no other way than his who was the Way!

> If anyone wishes to come after me, he must deny himself, and take up his cross daily and follow me. For whoever wishes to save his life will lose it, but whoever loses his life for my sake will save it (*Luke* 9: 23).

It is the dynamic called for in Christian Baptism:

> Are you not aware that you who were baptized into Christ Jesus were baptized into his death? You were buried with him. The old self has died (*Romans* 6: 3-5).

I have chosen a particular time of my life to share with you: the summer of 1973. Two summers before I was ordained to the priesthood, I kept a journal of myself and my attempts at ministry when I was stationed at the Church of St. Francis of Assisi. It's the story of how I lived Kenosis right in the heart of the capital of the world: New York City. What better place to check this out than in one of the busiest churches in the world? One block from Madison Square Garden and Penn Station, two blocks from Gimbel's and Macy's.

This is a theological reflection on that experience, through which I hope to grow as a person, as a Christian, and as a minister. I invite you, the reader, to go through that summer with me, and to use me as one person's experience of Kenosis, and so to use me as a prism to reflect about your own life journey of love.

My prayer is that in reflecting with me on my Kenosis, you may be plunged more deeply into the discovery of the areas in your life where you resist letting go. Dying to self, self-emptying, could be a doorway for you as it was and is for me, a doorway to becoming more free, to living more completely in the attitude of Christ Jesus the liberator. He's the One I follow, because he's the One who unlocked the ultimate mystery of life, death, by walking through its painful, frightening doors, embracing it totally, promising those who died with him will also do the same. Through love we pass from death to life; we share in his Resurrection and new life, becoming brand new creatures ourselves!

Yes, St. Francis was on to something! He found the secret. I think I have! "Plainly and simply," I hope you do.

FINDING THE PRISM OF KENOSIS

Every Christian grows up alongside the mystery of the cross. When a friar receives the habit of St. Francis, shaped in the form of a cross, he hears the words:

> God forbid that I should glory save in the cross of Our Lord Jesus Christ. Through it I am crucified to the world, and the world is crucified to me (*Gal.* 6: 14).

Yes, we all hear these words, and think we agree with them, as well as all those that have to do with "taking up the cross everyday and following in his footsteps." Yet, until these words are *owned*, until a breakthrough happens in someone's vision and mind, which convinces one of their ultimate value and truth, they remain just words, perhaps just pious clichés.

I began to find my way to Kenosis when I heard one of the finest American theologians, Regis Duffy, O.F.M., declare that any genuine renewal in the Church must come from a rediscovery of the cross. Francis of Assisi knew that, as did all those who were part of the early Franciscan movement. They helped to "rebuild the Church" in the Middle Ages. I believe that any refounding, rebuilding, renewing today must come from that very same discovery.

The Word Itself

I refer throughout this book to the word Kenosis as a noun. The word Kenosis comes from the Greek verb used in *Philippians* 2: 7. Here is a list of some different Bibles with different translations:

> *The New American Bible*: "he emptied himself."
> *The Living Bible*: "he laid down his mighty power and glory."
> *New International Version*: "he made himself nothing."
> *Today's English Version*: "he gave up all he had."

Translate it any way you wish as you read through, and perhaps the different wording will enrich the meaning for you. I hope that it does. And I hope that the rediscovery of Kenosis may help bring forth the renewal of the world, the Church, American society, married life, religious life, and the life of every searching, courageous individual!

Faith Seeking Understanding

As forementioned, I had always believed in the cross, but it wasn't until I studied theology that I found my prism. I grew into a change of mind. I'd like to share with you how I arrived at my understanding of Kenosis through my pursuit of theology. Here is what led me to my prism.

I feel that Kenosis is central in any concept of ministry.

If there is any sentence in the Gospel that expresses in a very concentrated way everything I have tried to say in the five chapters of this book (*Creative Ministry*), it is the sentence spoken by Jesus to his Apostles the day before His death: "A man can have no greater love than to lay down his life for his friends." (*John* 15: 13). For me these words summarize the meaning of all Christian ministry.[2]

Although Nouwen here is not quoting the verse from Philippians which precisely uses the word Kenosis, I think that he is referring to that basic notion essential to Christian life—emptying oneself, laying down one's life, being a person for others, loving, giving of oneself, letting go—all of which Jesus did in a redemptive way.

When I was preparing myself for the exemplification of Kenosis in my life, I acquired many insights through studying the Old Testament prophets. Prophets, as the conscience of Israel, often spoke plainly for God. The later prophets, however, seemed to be much more explicitly messianic.

As the prophetic role developed, there seemed to come a turning point, in Jeremiah and Isaiah, from the previous prophets. These men began to see their personal suffering as a redemptive aspect of declaring God's message. All the prophets had to suffer for their declarations. Prophets are very seldom popular. But it seems that Jeremiah began to prophesy about the Messiah as *Ebed Yahweh*, as the suffering servant, while he was really speaking through his own suffering as a reference, his own context, and of Israel as a people among the nations (*Jeremiah* 12: 19).

> During Israel's Babylonian exile, when away from the Temple, they discovered a new type of sacrifice—martyrdom. Cultic sacrifice was now superceded by a human's self-surrender.

Betz goes on to tell us:

> that Christ's sacrifice is not to be understood primarily in terms of ritual sacrifice, but in terms of martyrdom; it is a person's total offering of self.[3]

Sacrifice and how the covenant was expressed began to be understood as intimately connected with personal input and suffering, the self-offering of individuals.

> The Suffering Servant is said to have born the sins of many (*Isaiah* 53: 13), and thus to have made them righteous

(*Isaiah* 53: 11). Moreover, in Isaiah, the concept of the Suffering Servant is linked up closely with the covenant (*Isaiah* 42: 6, 49: 8). Thus the prophetic concept of the covenant is deepened and enriched.

The future covenant (prefigured in these prophets) is no longer rooted in an interiorization of the law, but in the vicarious love of the Servant who suffers on behalf of all.[4]

And so, it seems to me that the life of the minister (prophet) had implications on the development of the notions of sacrifice and covenant. Their lives also seemed to be rich prototypes, deep symbols, corporeal personalities of Israel, and foreshadowings of the future Messiah.

What these learnings did for me was to point me in the direction of a Christological model as a model for ministry. This model was the redemptive incarnational model of the Suffering Servant, particularly implying the notion of Kenosis, especially as celebrated by the early Christians in the Christological Hymn:

have the same mind of Christ Jesus, who did not cling to his divinity, but emptied himself, and took the form of a slave, being born in the likeness of men (*Phil.* 2: 6–11).

If Kenosis seems to be at the very heart of Christ, it certainly cannot be far from the core of the church, not to mention it as being essential for pastoral ministry, since Jesus Christ was *the* pastoral minister.

So, I began formulating this theological direction which became concretized in the prophetic ministry of the Old Testament. This not only gave me my concreteness, but also the particular phenomenon to describe, not myself as prophet, but as a minister. I have principles of Christology which would have implications for ecclesiology and pastoral ministry. Now I had found also the particular departure point for examining these principles, one man, a minister: myself.

In summary, I found the prism of Kenosis based on the Christological redemptive incarnational model, begun in the Suffering Servant motif in the Old Testament, continued and celebrated in the primitive life of the early Church. And I have chosen it as my prism because I feel that it is central for human, Christian, ecclesial life. Since I feel that the minister embodies the corporate personality of every Christian and of church life, Kenosis would seem to be central for ministerial life.

One might say that part of my approach is Heideggerian. As he studied *dasein* to discover more of *sein*, as he examined one being, man, or "being there" to somehow come to know something of "being" itself, so it is my hope that by looking at and discovering how one man—myself—as minister, attempts to live Kenosis, that somehow I will receive insights into what was the Kenosis of Jesus Christ, and hopefully to discover implications for the life of humanity, for the members of the Church, but particularly for those who serve in it and those who take it seriously.

Since I consider Kenosis as the core of Christ's life and, there-fore, as the core of Christian life, I equate ministry with Kenosis; for if one is truly a loving person, if one is self-emptying, self-offering for others, one cannot be far from the Master, "by whose wounds we were healed" (*Isaiah* 53: 5), who himself is the "way, the truth and the life" of all pastoral ministry.

Ministry as Kenosis

As I previously stated, since I equate ministry with Kenosis, this book will deal with how the minister deals with Kenosis in the significant relationships of his personality. The major part will consider the pastoral experience itself in chapter four. However, because the personal integration of the minister affects how he will minister, I have decided to deal with the minister, his attitudes, his relationship to God, himself, and his religious community, in chapters one, two, and three, respectively, in order to explore what it is he will bring to his ministry to others.

> The most important ingredient in this work (ministry) is the person of the pastor himself. The only self that can be employed in the relationships that constitute pastoral work is the genuine self. This cannot be revealed if it is not under-stood and accepted by the priest himself. Before the pastor can reconcile others to God, he must reconcile himself sym-pathetically to his own person.[5]

And so each chapter will explore a different Kenosis.

Chapter one: God/Self Kenosis
Chapter two: Self/Self Kenosis

Chapter three: Community/Self Kenosis
Chapter four: Others/Self Kenosis

I would like to emphasize different expressions of Kenosis in each chapter. The resolution of Kenosis in chapter one uncovers the "being" dimension of the minister, who he is. Chapter two discusses the "believing" side of the minister, how he believes in himself. Chapter three explores the "living" dimensions of Kenosis, the daily life of the minister with his brothers. Chapter four deals with the "serving" aspect of Kenosis, how the minister shares who he is, what he believes, and how he lives with the world around him.

Each chapter will follow a similar format. I will introduce each Kenosis by mentioning the theological, theoretical dimensions of it, along with the practical, dynamic dimensions of it. Examples from experiences then will be introduced which are either concrete descriptions of the pastoral experience or preconsiderations germane to it.

By means of analysis and critical evaluation, I will then discuss my areas of resistance to each particular Kenosis. Here I will indicate ongoing or potential difficulties, how I might be holding back from Kenosis, or true ministerial attitudes or practice in these particular areas.

Implications of the above and new understandings then will be discussed with their theological and professional ramifications.

SERVING IN THE HUB OF THE CITY

From the earliest days of the Franciscan Order, the Friars Minor have attempted to bring the Good News into the marketplace. These men are not monks, but troubadours of Jesus, as was Francis, not locked up in monasteries, but right smack in the middle of cities, towns, and villages. From the early days of the Order, even up until the 1950s the worldwide headquarters of the Order of Friars Minor was in the middle of Rome, Ara Coeli, near the Roman Forum and Senate, now the site of the tomb of Victor Emmanuel, the father of modern Italy. The friar's place is where the people are, and especially where the poor and needy are. From watching the free–spirited Friar Tuck in *Robin Hood* on television,

I believe I found the roots of my own Franciscan vocation.

About seventy-five years ago, the Franciscans of Holy Name Province invented the idea of a service church. The service church attempts to be a center in cities where the needs of the people can be met by the friars' availability. These churches, conducted by the friars, exist in New York City, Boston, Providence, New Bedford, Chicago, Hartford, Wilmington, and Greensboro. It is called a "service church" by the friars because a variety of services are offered to the people: Confessions are available all day long; ten to fifteen Masses are scheduled daily at convenient times for shoppers, workers, visitors, and businesspeople in downtown areas.

Friars are likewise available for consultations of many kinds. Popular devotions are conducted at different times each week to minister to the piety of the faithful. The personality of the particular church reflects the talents of the friars there as well as their perceptions of the current needs of the people in their city.

Heart and Soul

Cronan Kelly, O.F.M., once described "31st Street" the way the friars refer to St. Francis, as "a small little heartbeat in the middle of New York." I'd say that it exists in fulfillment of the words of Pope John Paul II when he spoke in Battery Park on his papal visit: "You must remind the city that it has a soul." Heart and soul in our cities!

Because of their central location and availability, the service churches are convenient meeting places for many self-help groups in the cities. As a special priority, the friars and lay staff also conduct popular adult education programs at convenient times on the latest issues in theology, spirituality, social justice, church and world affairs.

One could mention numerous outreach programs or individual apostolates carried on by particular friars, but I will discuss in this book only those engaged in by the community at large, or those in which I myself was involved.

One of my supervisors, Fr. John McVean, works with the staff of a welfare hotel, The Aberdeen Hotel, on 32nd Street, which is also a halfway house for Bellevue Hospital. Fr. McVean and a few other friars also work on a weekly basis with a program of senior citizens based at St. Francis. Within the past several years, Fr. McVean, Fr. John Felice, and Fr. Tom Walters opened three St. Francis residences, most successful in their care for welfare residents who are socially or emotionally handicapped. Every morning since 1930, the friars have conducted a breadline which feeds approximately 350–400 men daily. The secular Franciscans at St. Francis also run a bookshop and a gift shop. Approximately forty-five friars are involved in the ministry of the service church itself. About forty other friars were in residence, some of whom worked at the Provincial Headquarters (which was at St. Francis then); others worked for either the Franciscan Missionary Union or the Franciscan Family Circle Pilgrimages. About ten friars were either retired or semi-retired. There also were several student friars.

It was here in the midst of all this activity that I examined very carefully and in depth my experience of Kenosis. I hope you find it as interesting as I did.

My Program

The depth of my pastoral experience here came not so much from doing one particular apostolate or ministry with intensity, but from both the variety of people and the experiences I encountered.

Along with two other student friars from Washington, DC and one novice from Brookline, Massachusetts, I was stationed at St. Francis from June until August, 1973. I was there to pursue my in-depth pastoral experience, while the others were to experience the life and ministry at St. Francis.

Each of us had an individual friar-supervisor with whom we met for at least one hour per week. We assembled together for a group discussion with our supervisors for one to two hours per week. We celebrated a small group liturgy on a weekly basis, and also prayed daily with the community.

Each of us was placed on the work schedule according to his own talents and capabilities, considering personalities and the individual's interests in the ministry.

The following is an example of my weekly schedule, including a brief explanation of what the duty might entail:

Monday: Free day.

Tuesday: As an acolyte, I helped distribute Communion at the 10:00, 11:15, 12:15 Masses.

From 2:00 P.M.–8.00 P.M., Parlor duty. If anyone wanted to consult with a friar and didn't specifically need or request a priest, I would speak with that person after explaining that I was not a priest. More details and examples of such experiences will be included in later chapters, as well as my reflections on them.

Wednesday: 9:00 A.M.–12:00 noon, 3:00–6:00 P.M., Information desk. Assignment at the information desk in the church office during these hours included administering Mass cards, consoling bereaved people who were procuring the cards, having religious articles blessed, making referrals, giving information about when certain friars had assignments, distributing clothes and small amounts of money to the poor, and receiving money and clothing from people as donations.

2:00–3:00 P.M., Supervisory meeting with Fr. Blaise Hamaday.

8:00 P.M., Group supervisory meeting and discussion.

Thursday: 6:45–7:30 A.M., Breadline. This consisted of greeting the poor men and women, keeping the line orderly, preventing fights, giving out sandwiches as well as clothing to those who requested it.

9:00 A.M.–12 noon, Aberdeen Hotel. On these mornings I walked two blocks to 32nd Street with Fr. McVean. The tenants at the Aberdeen Hotel had one apartment which they used as a social center or recreation room. On Thursday mornings, coffee and donuts were provided, and the residents were urged to socialize. I spoke with and listened to the tenants during the morning.

1:00 P.M.–4:30 P.M., Senior citizens' program. Other friars and I set up and took down tables and chairs for our 150 senior citizens. We mingled with them, and sometimes entertained with singing or skits. We prepared and distributed small food packets and served coffee and tea.

5:15 P.M., Small group liturgy, to which all in the community were invited, but which usually consisted of us student friars, our supervisors, and one or two other friars.

Friday: Communions 10:00, 11:15, 12:15 masses. 2:00–8:00 P.M., Parlor duty or Information desk. 1:00–3:00 P.M., 4:00–6:00 P.M., 8:00–10:00 P.M., Homily preparation for weekend.

Saturday: 9:00 A.M.–12:00 Noon, Information desk. 2:00–3:00 P.M., Homily preparation. 4:00–5:00 P.M., Led singing, served as commentator, lector, preacher, distributor of Communion at Mass.

Sunday: 6:45 A.M., Breadline, 11:00 A.M. Mass, at which I might serve as lector commentator, possibly preach, distribute Communion. 12:00 noon, Mass at which I distributed Communion. Afternoon, beginning of Monday free day.

Self-Initiated Activities: At different times when I was not occupied, in between schedule-work, or in waiting for a parlor call, I often stood outside the church in my religious habit and met, greeted, and spoke with people.

On at least two evenings, I went down the street to Madison Square Garden in my Franciscan habit and talked with teenagers who were waiting for a concert to begin.

I also attended a weekly charismatic prayer meeting on Thursday evenings.

My Initial Goals

Plainly, simply, I had two initial goals: to be a learner, and to explore and experience Kenosis.

My goal in the program was more on an operative level than on a productive one. I was interested in growth, learning through reflection. I wanted to observe something of the friars' ministry and how they lived at St. Francis. I sought to grow in my relationship to Jesus Christ, his Church, my brothers, and myself. Through this learning and growth, I wished to become a holier, a more effective, more competent, more professional minister of the Gospel.

Contrary to the attitudes I have entertained in the past toward the apostolate, I wasn't interested in going to St. Francis to change the whole apostolate to my liking. No, I was there not so much to contribute as to receive, to learn, to assimilate, to appreciate. My usual motivation is to improve and change things as, for example, in my community life and apostolate in Washington, DC. I found that this new approach for me this summer was not only adventurous, but a truly refreshing change. Somehow, with this newly adopted attitude I became freer and more open. I found myself expecting less, appreciating more, criticizing less, and tolerating more.

I wanted to experience Kenosis as deeply as possible, by doing it and reflecting upon it. In experiencing Kenosis, I felt that I would somehow come to know a bit more of the mystery that is Christ, that is God. In emptying myself, giving myself to others, I might become more like Jesus and therefore, might become a more effective minister, a better friar, a more authentic Catholic, and a fuller, much more human being.

One might have a million experiences in life, but if one does not reflect on his or her experiences, there would be little or no growth. My method in writing this book will flow from the personal integration of my theological knowledge, aided by all of my past studies in philosophy and psychology, as well as everything I've ever learned in my life. It will be grounded in my lived, concrete experience as a professed believer, a Friar Minor, a pastoral minister at the Church of St. Francis in New York City.

CHAPTER 1

God/Self Kenosis: Being

Deus Meus et Omnia!
My God and my All!

—*Little Flowers of St. Francis, Omnibus*

Who are you, O God, Most High?
and what am I?

—*Little Flowers of St. Francis, Omnibus*

Abba John of Thebaid said: Above all things a monk ought to be humble. In fact, this is the first commandment of the Savior who said: Blessed are the poor in spirit, for theirs is the kingdom of heaven.

—Nomura Yushi, *Desert Wisdom*

Blessed is the servant of God who esteems himself no better when he is praised and exalted by people than when he is considered worthless, simple, and despicable; for what one is before God, that he is and nothing more.

—Admonitions XIX, *Francis and Clare*

Blessed is the servant who attributes every good to the Lord God!

—Admonitions XVIII, *Francis and Clare*

THE ANT STORY

One afternoon while I was reading the Good News, I came across the phrase in Matthew where Jesus said: "If you have faith the size of a mustard seed you could say to this mountain, hurl yourself into the sea and it would happen."

I left the chapel and went to my favorite meditation spot overlooking a sunset on a vast field, and sat there on "my rock." I asked the Lord to please tell me what he meant by this.

As I sat there on my rock, I looked down at another large rock where I used to comfortably place my feet. It was a slanted rock, kind of on its side. As I continued to reflect and seek the meaning of the Lord's words about the mountain and faith, I looked down where I was going to place my feet and noticed a tiny ant trying to crawl up to the top of this rock, up the hilly slanted side. I was fascinated watching it, because it seemed that every two steps the little ant gained it slid down three or four steps. I also noticed that the ant was carrying something, perhaps his supper or another little ant.

I said to the ant, "If you want me to, I can pick you up and put you wherever you want to go, and it would be a cinch for me! It would be a piece of cake! I'm so much bigger and more powerful than you! But I won't do it unless you ask me to." The Lord answered my seeking question about moving the mountains through my friend, the little ant.

It was only later, after further reflection, that I discovered there was more for me here. I realized that the little ant would have been happier if I had become a little ant and showed it how to best be an ant, or helped it to climb up the mountain as Jesus did for us in the Incarnation.

WILL THE REAL GOD IN MY LIFE PLEASE STAND UP?

Perhaps the problem of the God/Self Kenosis can best be expressed by a brief excerpt from *Gaudium et Spes*, Vatican II's *Pastoral Constitution of the Church in the Modern World*:

No doubt today's progress in science and technology can foster a certain exclusive emphasis on observable data and an agnosticism about everything else. The danger exists that humans, confiding too much in modern discoveries, may even think that they are sufficient unto themselves, and no longer seek any higher realities.[1]

I think that we often like to perceive ourselves as sufficient, not needing a God. We certainly do it enough! This, however, is what I consider to be the most basic Kenosis called for in human life, for one to admit that s/he is not God! It seems to me to be one of the definite effects of original sin that a human considers oneself as God, or acts as if one is God. Part of the mystery is that God made us in God's image and likeness, made us so wonderfully that we can even consider ourselves to be God or to be even greater than God, or not to even need God.

I call this the "God Game." One of life's challenges is finding out who our true god is, whom we worship and live for, not the One we *say* we worship on Sunday, but the real force that runs our lives. Who or what consciously or unconsciously rules our lives? Who or what is our "bottom line?" To resolve the God Game or complete it, each of us must answer the sublime question from our very depths and with frightening honesty: "Will the real god in my life please stand up?"

Ministry has caused me to ask basic questions concerning my own human existence. "Am I God?" happens to be one of them. I feel that the honest resolution of this question will result in perhaps the most basic Kenosis called for in the life of faith.

The ramifications of this resolution will have definite influence on one's effectiveness in ministry because the resolution will affirm if one is truly self-emptying and working for God's glory and Kingdom, or if one is boosting one's own ego and building one's own kingdom under the aegis of religion.

When one does resolve this Kenosis and truly worships the living God, not some manifestation of one's own ego, one can become free from competition with other people for supremacy (being the controller or godfather). Then one can become equal with other people as brothers and sisters of the one Father. When one discovers that s/he is not God, and discovers who God truly is, that person can become free to be human again. When a person finds out who God is, s/he learns who s/he is. Or at least, through my experience, when one finds out at last that s/he is not God, s/he then can become free to discover who s/he really is. S/he can stop playing the game the wrong way and just be human. Trying to be God can be an awful lot of work! Humans do a poor job pulling it off. We usually become hateful creatures, to both ourselves and others. Hitler is an example. I believe he eventually killed himself. He detested himself at the end. Am I ever Hitler in my own world? Who or what I worship shows. I start to become it. What am I becoming?

Not God, But Who?

When we discover we are not God, we become painfully aware of our limitedness, our finiteness, our humanness. We become aware that the initial/basic stance towards the Ultimate Other is one of response and reception. We become aware of our sinfulness; imperfection; and pilgrim-like, incomplete status. We realize our impotency, our ungodness.

We then can begin to discover God as Creator, as both First Cause and Continual Cause, as Judge, as the Center of life, rather than ourselves. How hard it is to really do this!

This Kenosis is not resolved once, but is ongoing. There may be one or more dramatic resolutions, but these must continually be remade. This is indeed one of the built-in frustrations of this imperfection in us humans. I cannot even acknowledge myself not to be God perfectly! I will never totally empty myself of the desire and temptation to be God in my own little world. I imagine this is merely another manifestation of God being God and humans being human. Part of this Kenosis is realizing and accepting the fact that we, as humans, will always be developing and in process.

This I believe to be the original sin, which is not wiped away magically with a zapping at Baptism. It is not washed away by pouring some water, but with a lifetime of dying to self, by living life in the Church, living out and constantly remaking our baptismal vows. As St. Paul reminds us in *Romans* 6: 4, ''we were buried with him . . . our old self has died.''

Letting Go of Ego

After going to many prayer meetings where "Jesus is Lord" is a constant theme of the singing, praying, and exhorting, I think that I finally came to a true commitment and ongoing realization of my need to admit this, that "Jesus is Lord" of my own life—not only with my lips, but in my heart. This forced me to give up some of my ego and self-dependence, and to surrender more to the Lord.

On another occasion, when I participated in a week of prayer with other friars, I came to a startling realization of my sinfulness. We were sharing reflections on the scripture about Peter not wanting to cast out the nets after a day of no fish. I had been feeling that way—useless—with the clientele who came to St. Francis after my first few weeks there, and I was tempted to give up. This sharing inspired me to hear the Lord's Will, not my own, and to throw my net out again, simply because he told me to.

Often in the apostolate I met people to whom I was personally attracted. One such young man was a collegian from Colombia. He was involved in a faith crisis. I was tempted to develop a friendship with this person, rather than to minister to him in his relationship to the Lord. This situation again made me ask myself who my real God was and who was I serving, God or myself? Not that friendship would have been bad, but a little too much of Kevin's need was there, rather than the other's. He was clearly looking for God. I wanted to show him me. This and other truths continually need to be relearned by me. My learnings are cyclic, periodic, and ongoing—never done.

Resistance

We must continually evaluate how and whether we truly are emptying ourselves in our relationship to God in the way that this Kenosis calls for.

I found myself replaying my role as God in many subtle but real ways. There are often periods in my life when I sit back and stop learning, close up my desire to grow, simply because I think at that time that I know all there is to know. Or, I'm too lazy or tired!

As a minister, it is easy to become the almighty judge and righteous one, forgetting one's own sinfulness. One often can make one's own narrow perception the criterion for what everyone else should think, do, or be. Hitler did this in the most extreme way. People in authority and in ministry, whether they like it or not, are viewed with respect by the public and are often most prone to this pitfall.

When serving people, I often found myself almost forgetting that I was an agent of Someone Greater; I forgot to depend on God, thinking everything depended on me and my power, rather than on the Lord's, that His grace alone is sufficient. Other times I found myself running out of spiritual energy because I hadn't been truly united with Jesus in prayer. I forgot that unless I remained united with him I would not bear any fruit (*John* 15: 5).

How I came across or looked was sometimes more important to me than the Lord's work. Jesus is the Vine. I am only a branch. Other occasions arose where my pride and my need for success seemed more important than any desire to serve the Master.

These areas of resistance seem to me to be constant problems in ministry because they stem from the stubbornness of one's ego to deny completely that one is not God. The problem keeps popping up. It seems peculiar that even as a minister, I am often in conflict with the God I profess to be serving. Perhaps that is why Jesus was always on the case of the "holy people" of his day. Occupational hazard—beware!

Ramifications for Ministry

Facing the reality of this Kenosis has helped me to face my own limited power in ministry. I can only do so much. Much depends on God's Will and His Grace to bring healing or blessing to ministerial endeavors. This realization is a real faith dimension.

Christian ministers ideally work together for the same end: God's glory and the establishment of the Kingdom. However, I have learned that "one plants, another waters, but God alone provides the growth" (1 *Cor.* 3: 7). One minister might spend years planting seeds for spiritual growth in others. Another may come and reap after God has blessed. I have experienced both. I have learned that God has his own Plan, and his own timetable.

One minister can struggle for a certain end for many years, but "unless the Lord build the house, they labor in vain who build it" (*Psalms* 127: 1).

The Kingdom of God is like a mustard seed. God's Word takes time to develop in people. Ministers must wait in hope for the proper time to reap. They must learn to respect how time, and God's Grace, plus people's receptiveness all jell to bring about the desired results for the Lord.

Personal Limits/Learnings

From the realization of my limitations as a person, I have come to face the fact that there will be, as there have been, many problems I cannot solve. I don't have to.

Even if I were the greatest counselor in the world, there would come times when I personally would not be able to help someone simply because of some personal or professional inadequacy on my part. This has reminded me of the need for referral. As a minister, I should know to whom I can refer cases which I am incapable of handling. I must admit my limits with a person, and not seek to hold on to that person if I am of no real professional use to him or her. I may not be the Lord's needed instrument in a particular situation. Can I give up my messianic need to save everyone?

On the other side of the coin, I learned that I can do a lot more for people than I thought, simply by showing concern, listening, and supporting them. I learned that often concern is what people need more than an answer to a specific problem or dilemma. Here is where the wisdom of everyone's favorite friar struck me. John Bosco, O.F.M., who modeled for the friar cookie jar, says often to people: "I may not be able to help you, but I'm not going to hurt you."

Letting God Be God

As part of our tendency towards pride, independence, self-sufficiency, and playing the role of God, Original Sin will always be with us in our human nature. The challenge of the God/Self Kenosis is to admit and accept one's limitations during dramatic moments of decisiveness. But also, one is challenged as a minister of God to continually remake this option to work for God rather than for oneself. The minister must constantly strive in his life to be less self-centered, less judgmental, less anxious about his own input into ministry, and more dependent on God's grace. The minister must always be careful not to become his own cause, under the guise of religion. I think that this latter problem is a very real one, although subtle, in ministry. Ministers can often use God for their own name, fame, or glory.

Perhaps the worst sin is if a minister does not do his own homework on his own life. One can hide in religion, inflicting one's own hang-ups, hurts, and unresolved conflicts on others—and get away with it! If a servant does not deal with his own ungodliness, or shadow, the people of God often get "stuck" with it and have very little recourse.

St. Paul's letter to the Corinthians best states for me my role in relationship to God, taking into account my limitation, imperfection, and humanity. This small phrase gets to the very heart of the Kenosis called for in the God/Self relationship. We, as humans, are common clay pots, earthen vessels.

> This priceless treasure we hold in common clay pots, to show that the splendid power of it, belongs to God not to us (2 *Cor.* 4: 7).

If the minister can keep his common "clay-potness" in mind, his humanness, and not set himself up as God, then God can work through him; and the Lord's splendor, his "priceless treasure," will be revealed through the humanity of the minister. Things seem to work best when God is God, and humans are human.

God has been God for an awfully long time! He does it very well! He really knows how to be God! If we humans could only learn to let God be God, and to let God be as great as God really is! We could become what we were meant to be. We could do what we were meant to do. I believe that Mary of Nazareth and Francis of Assisi knew this secret. Look what happened. The Blessed Mother of Jesus in her *Magnificat* exclaimed:

> My whole being proclaims the greatness of the Lord. God who is mighty has done great things for me, Holy is God's Name. (*Luke* 1: 46, 49).

She, as queen of the little ones, the poor of Yahweh, the *anawim* of the Hebrews, could acknowledge her total dependence on the great and wonderful God in whom she trusted. "Being deeply troubled in spirit," her reply to the words and invitation of the Angel Gabriel was her ultimate self-surrendering statement, her *fiat*:

> I am the servant of the Lord. Let it be done to me as you say (*Luke* 1: 39).

St. Francis of Assisi, perhaps the richest poorman that ever lived and the maddest wiseman as well, could pray and truly live as if he meant his famous words, the motto of the Franciscan Order: "My God and My All!"

It is such a relief to just be human, and not God! It is sad that so few ever get to this level, even those in religion. Too many act like they have to be perfect. In the Penance Rite, every Eucharist begins with this realization, remembering our humanness, our limits, our sin, reminding ourselves of "who I am before God, that I am, and nothing more." And again, before partaking of that great treasure of the Bread that is Jesus: "Lord, I am not worthy to receive you, but only say the word."

Let Go, Let God

Most self-help Twelve Step programs see this Kenosis that I've talked about as Step One: Acknowledging a Higher Power, one greater than oneself, however one might conceive it. The quick phrase that is used in Alcoholics Anonymous is: "Let go, let God!" I believe this to be the very beginning of all spiritual beginnings, letting God be God!

Last year during Lent, I read about the risk of letting go.

> The act of letting go can be seen as a sign of either despair or trust. Consider the picture of someone hanging on with both hands. If you imagine the person to be twenty floors above the ground hanging onto a window sill, letting go is a sign of exhaustion, of giving up. If, on the other hand, you imagine the person to be a child hanging from a low branch of an apple tree while her father waits with open arms to catch her, letting go is a sign of freedom and trust.[2]

CHAPTER 2

Self/Self Kenosis: Believing

The fantastic thing about faith is:
not so much my belief in God,
but God's belief in me.

—Kevin Cronin's Journal

You are the light of the world!
You are the salt of the earth!

—Jesus, to us

Brother Leo, in whatever way it seems best to you to please the Lord God and to follow in his footprints and his poverty, do this, with the blessing of God and my obedience.

—Francis' Letter to Br. Leo, *Francis and Clare*

Therefore hold back nothing of yourselves for yourselves, so that he who gives himself totally to you may receive you totally.

—Francis' Letter to entire Order of Friars Minor,
Francis and Clare

No matter where they are, the friars must always remember that they have given themselves up completely and handed over their whole selves to our Lord Jesus Christ.

— O.F.M. Rule of 1221 *Omnibus*

THE BILLY STORY

I used to spend some of my vacations at my sister Ronnie's house on Long Island, not far from where I grew up. I enjoyed visiting her, her husband Ron, and her three sons, Eddie, Billy, and Bobby. Not having any children of my own, I enjoyed the family atmosphere.

I have a special relationship with all my nieces and nephews, because they are all unique. However, Billy was my godson, and so he was somehow a little extra special. I think he felt it too.

I would often take the boys to the candy store, the movies, to church, or to walk the dog. Billy was so cute, with red hair and freckles, and kind of an imp. One day when he was five we were walking and he bent down to pick up something he found by the curb in the street. He was so excited! It was a dime! Then it meant something. Billy was so happy dreaming about all he could do with his new found treasure. He was the happiest boy in the world.

A thought came across my mind to teach Billy a lesson. I reached in my pocket for a dollar bill. I showed it to Billy and asked him if he would like to trade me his dime for my dollar? He looked at the dime. He looked at my dollar. The dime was so bright and shiny. He held it tight. It was his! His treasure! He looked back at the dollar. "Uh-uh! Uncle Kev, I want my dime!"

"Billy," I said, "you could trade this dollar in for ten more dimes. What I have for you is ten times more and better than that dime!" He looked at both again, enjoying his shiny dime, looking me in the eyes, and said once more, "No, Uncle Kev, I want my dime."

I guess Billy realized that if he wanted the dollar he had to let go of the dime. It was a trade! As much as he loved me and trusted me, he couldn't or wouldn't let go.

WONDERFULLY MADE

As was chapter one, chapter two is a preliminary insight into the self of the minister. In knowing and learning what a minister is like in himself, I think one can get a fair idea of how a minister will function in service to people. I invoke the Latin expression *agere sequitur esse*, "doing follows being."

As a person is faced with the reality of one's humanity, of one's ungodliness, of one's limitation and imperfection, one might say: "Why bother living? I'm nobody! It is not even worth trying! If I can't be on top, perfect, or God, then I won't try at all." The "all or nothing" attitude is so often the cop out of today. Here is where the second Kenosis is called for. It takes tremendous courage to be just a human being! A person is challenged to believe, to believe that even in one's sinful limited condition, as an earthen vessel, that one has worth because one is loved by God! For God loved us and continues to love us as we are:

> At the appointed time, when we were still powerless, Christ died for us godless people. It is rare that anyone should lay down his life for a just person, though it is barely possible that for a good person someone may have the courage to die. It is precisely in this that God proves his love for us: that while we were still sinners, Christ died for us (*Romans* 5: 6–9).

God made us! We are extensions of God, manifestations of God's life-giving nature! We are good! Because I receive this love, this empowers and enables me to consider myself worthwhile and lovable. For God thought I was worth it. He knew me from my mother's womb. God believed in me from the very start. God thought enough of me to create me!

> Truly you have formed my inmost being; you knit me in my mother's womb. I give you thanks that I am fearfully, wonderfully made; wonderful are your works! My soul also you knew full well; nor was my frame unknown to you when I was made in secret, when I was fashioned in the depths of the earth (*Psalm* 139: 13–15).

God counts on me to do something wonderful with the time God has given to me. All life, all time, belong to God! God owns it all, and loans it out and expects it back one day with interest. That's the most fantastic thing about faith to me—not my belief in God, but that God believes in me, and trusts me with his precious gift of time and life! Even though "my days were limited before one of them existed" (*Psalm* 139: 16), I am indeed wonderfully made. And I am worth dying for. Jesus thought so. Being fully alive glorifies God!

I Am Special

"You are the light of the world. You are the salt of the earth" (*Matt.* 5: 13–14) tells me that Jesus saw in sinners potential for growth. In those hand-picked first twelve simple men Jesus saw great potential! It seems to me that God believes in us, writes straight with crooked lines.

The Lord Jesus loved his disciples and through his creative love called them to greatness. His faith in them, despite their personal weaknesses, seemed to give them the courage to become great people, men who could believe that they had something to offer. He enabled them!

Jesus seems to tell us through the parable of the different talents that every human is gifted with something special or with many special blessings for which each one of us will be accountable. Each person must use, must celebrate the talents the Lord has given. How harsh the Lord will be on those who hide them and refuse to use them, putting them under a bushel, or "out of fear, burying them in the ground" (*Matt.* 25).

From this Scripture, and from many books I have read, it seems clear to me that each person must accept herself, himself, with her/his own abilities and lovableness, gifts and talents. Why else would the Lord have made this love a criterion for one of the great commandments, "to love your neighbor as you love yourself" (*Matt.* 22: 39)?

I don't think in this Holy Word that Jesus was so much giving a commandment about how much we should love the neighbor, I think he was telling us how much we would: as I love myself. I have learned that to the degree I care for, love, and cherish the self God has given me, to this degree I am capable of loving another.

Unfortunately, some people have made this commandment a dead end. They are still busy loving themselves, never getting to the second half of the commandment. Still involved in the narcissism that is so popular and acceptable in American culture, many have quoted these words of Jesus as an excuse to love only self. "When I'm done loving me perfectly or enough, then I'll get on with loving others." No wonder they never get to the second part!

Healthy self-love is a rare find. People are afraid of how it might look or seem to others if they honestly try to take good care of themselves. Yet, healthy self-love becomes one's capacity for healthy other-love. We treat those closest to us the way we treat ourselves, which often isn't very good. Sad to say, some of us wouldn't treat a dog as badly as we sometimes treat ourselves.

It cannot be: "I love me first, then I'll love others." It is a simultaneous process, not a first, then second step. The quality of other-love develops with the quality of self-love, and possibly vice versa. As a person, if I do not accept, love, believe in myself, how can I love others? Another Latin saying is: *Nemo dat quod non habet*, "Nobody gives what he doesn't have." Or more colloquially, "You can't give what you ain't got!"

And so we are faced with another form of Kenosis, believing in oneself. I think that it would be very comfortable, very easy, not to be responsible for one's own self. Often people who are sick or have problems get the reward of people's attention. It is more difficult to be healthy and responsible. It takes courage to believe in oneself!

I am believable because God who is good has made me in His Image (*Gen.* 1: 27). I am able. I am worthy. I am good. God who made me is good! God makes good things! God has become a man, and suffered and died for me. If for no other reason, because he has believed in me I must believe in myself, now in a knowledgeable and actual way, and in the future with hope of development, in a potential way.

This reminds me of a line from the movie *Brother Sun, Sister Moon*, by Franco Zefferelli, when Pope Innocent III says to the young Francis of Assisi in the Vatican: "In our preoccupation with Original Sin, we have often forgotten about original grace."

This self-emptying comes in knowing and accepting oneself as good and worthwhile in a believing way at the very core of one's being, in the form of an attitude of some degree of self-confidence, no matter what others think about it. There is an awful lot of pseudo self-confidence masquerading today, because it's a fad to be self-confident. This can display itself in aggressive, unchari- table, bulldozing behavior, supposedly "assertiveness."

This is not the kind of self-confidence I am talking about.

What do I have? What do I have to give?

As has been stated already, "Nobody can give what he does not have." Ministry has challenged me to face what it is I have to give. Ministry has invited me to see again who I am, in order that I might discover what it is, or who it is, that I might offer to others in loving service.

There seems to be a mutual relationship between Kenosis and ministry. That is, as I grow in my life with God my ministry becomes richer. And, as I grow in ministry, my relationship with God seems to improve. So, too, does my relationship to myself. As I believe more in myself, my ministry improves. And as my ministry improves, I believe more in myself.

Knowing ourselves means being open and honest with ourselves. We must take into account both our assets and foibles. We must not intentionally leave one stone unturned. We must seek to find where we are hiding from our true selves, regarding both our positive and negative qualities. Self-emptying challenges us to discover and become responsible for our own gifts and goodness. It demands also that we face how we try to ignore or defend ourselves from our negative attributes or our shadow-sides.

From what we know, both the positive and the negative, we ought to seek to discover the good qualities which we can nourish, give thanks for, and believe in. We might easily move from a reasonable faith in ourselves based on what we know, to a trusting confidence in ourselves, about the mystery of our persons which we do not know yet, or of which we are not 100 percent certain.

We must not hide from negative qualities, but emphasize those Godly, worthwhile, trustworthy qualities, "original goodness," which can make us seem credible to ourselves. This Kenosis is felt as we try to make a faith leap in ourselves before all the facts are in, saying "yes" to the mystery of our personalities, based on the reasonable faith we have in ourselves from our limited self-knowledge, "yes" to the unknown goodness within.

Growth seems to be a continual ongoing process, and of course, is integral to this Kenosis. I don't think that we ever make a total "yes" or faith leap in ourselves. There will always seem to be a creative tension between who we are, and who we would like to be, the real and ideal selves. Hopefully, this tension with a positive faith thrust will constantly call us to self-transcendence, to growth, to becoming more and more like the One in whose image all of us were made, the "will to believe" of William James.

How Am I Doing?

These examples will be in the form of positive and negative reactions from people and from myself, based on my performance in ministry.

I find that a very real challenge of this Kenosis is the ability to accept compliments. The pastor of St. Francis, at whose Mass I frequently commentated and led the singing, often told me how I really seemed to motivate the community to participate. Women often responded positively to my preaching, mentioning my sensitivity, warmth, and ability to communicate. Such comments were very encouraging and uplifting.

At times, friars criticized the "sing-songy" tone of my voice, or my poor use of the microphone. My supervisor helped me learn much through his negative criticism. He pointed out that I sometimes seemed to manipulate people who came for counseling. Even though I tried to be nondirective, he said I was often directive in an indirect way.

I noticed in myself that I usually feel confident of my good qualities but sometimes deny my negative ones. My supervisor helped me to realize that I tend to repress my frustrations rather than acknowledge them, and that I have some difficulty with authority, which I do not like to face. He told me how these feelings usually surface, whether I deal with them or not, either as a look on my face or a tone in my voice. It is very difficult for me to face my negative qualities. Here, again, is where Kenosis demands a certain death to self, in order to grow to new life.

Areas of Resistance

Again, these resistances are more or less preliminary considerations to ministry, existing in attitudes or actions of the minister.

At times, a minister might indulge in self-pity for a number of reasons, and convince himself of his lack of worth, even have what some call a "pity party." Poor me!

Or, one might try to disguise negative self-attitudes by an air of overconfidence, often expressed as exaggerated humor or bullying.

There is resistance when a person knows s/he can do something well, but hides behind the motivation "that I do not want to be noticed." At the cost of inauthenticity, s/he remains safe in false humility.

A minister can be unkenotic when he conducts his life at the whim of the audience. This might involve adapting negative attitudes in self-compromise to please others, or it might involve denying one's positive qualities in the presence of others who might either threaten one for, or be threatened by, those positive qualities.

CHARISM

One very real consideration regarding this Self/Self Kenosis has faced the Church since its foundation. That is the conflict, dialectic, complementation that exists between the institution and the individual charism.

When one believes in one's own charism, one must keep it purified in its realization and development within the Body of Christ. One must offer that charism, giftedness, believability, to the purification and edification of the Church. The gift is not for the individual alone, it belongs to the Body. It is within this Body of Christ, within obedience, that every charism must grow, be cultivated, and brought to completion. "To each person the manifestation of the Spirit is given for the common good" (1 *Cor.* 12: 7).

Another spiritual consideration has to do with one's own salvation, as the minister realizes his/her giftedness.

It's easy to get fanatically involved and overtaken by one's greatness in a bad sense. One can get caught up in one's own success. The recipient, in this way, just might miss the main reason for one's giftedness, one's own sanctification through it. I think of the Lord's words, applying them to this situation: "What does it profit a man if he gains the whole world, but suffers the loss of his own soul?" (*Mark* 8: 36).

All charisms have an inherent "not-yetness" in them. The person must know and accept where s/he is, but also in creative fidelity, must know and be committed to constant growth and development of his or her charism and personality for the sake of the Kingdom of God, which itself is in continual evolution and process to fulfillment.

Questions I often address to myself are: "Am I compulsive or charismatic?" "Why do I do things?" "What is my motivation?" "Is my motivation coming from an integrated self, or am I seeking to be faithful to a certain way of being because people expect it of me, and I need to put on this show of false pride?" "What am I proving?" "To whom?" "Why do I do what I do?" "Role playing or real self?"

Another professional insight gained from facing the self/self Kenosis is the awareness of moods, and how moods might affect ministry. I have come to realize that how I feel about myself at certain times will show in my preaching or counseling, whether I like it or not. If I don't deal with my emotions, they will deal with me!

Join the Human Race

Self-alienation seems to be a current, very popular way of expressing the chief manifestation of original sin in twentieth-century America. The flight to drugs, alcohol, and other escapes seems to indicate the human flight from self. One can easily find security in the escape of self-pity, under whatever guise chosen. However, I think that in order to become a human person, one has to overcome these negative attitudes towards self, these sinful attitudes, and one has to self-empty by seeing oneself honestly, accepting oneself, and attempting to grow. Welcome to the human race!

As a Christian and minister I can see no other way to live. I accept salvation, God loving me, and his manifestation of that salvation in my life.

I can give thanks, Eucharist. If I did not have some good feeling about myself, I doubt if I could be thankful. And I am thankful. The small Greek word *charis* in the middle of Eucharist means gift. Eucharist is the response of one who is a grateful receiver of gifts.

Not much real Eucharist happens if people don't realize how they've been gifted. No thanksgiving meals without grateful hearts! "Let us give thanks to the Lord our God! It is right to give God thanks and praise!"

Someone who is charismatic is someone with special gifts. That means we're all charismatic, because we're all gifted! When I see myself as gifted, I can see where I do fit into the Body of Christ, with all the other gifts (1 *Cor.* 13). We build up the Body, announcing the Kingdom and making it present in our world. I want to bear good fruit for the Lord, and so I think I must see to it that I am good (*Luke* 4: 43–45). And yet, I must not fear my limitedness, my weakness, whatever "thorn in the flesh" I might have, for as St. Paul tells us, this is to keep us

> from being puffed up and proud. And that in this weakness is when God's power is the strongest. For when I am weak, then I am strong (2 *Cor.* 12: 7–10).

> But, because we possess this ministry through God's mercy, we do not give in to discouragement (2 *Cor.* 4: 1).

And so I do not fear my weakness, which I am working on, nor do I desire to hide from the responsibility of my goodness.

> I do not claim that I have already succeeded in this, or have already become perfect; but I am racing to grasp the prize if possible, since I have been grasped by Christ Jesus. I do not think of myself as having reached the finish line. But I give no thought to what lies behind, but push on to what is ahead (*Phil.* 3: 12–13).

What I am saying is:

> Indeed the whole created world eagerly awaits the revelation of the sons and daughters of God! Yes, we know that all creation groans and is in agony even until now. It groans with the pain of childbirth. Not only that, but we ourselves groan inwardly, although we have the Spirit as first fruits, while we await the redemption of our bodies. Hoping for what we cannot see, means awaiting it with patient endurance (*Romans* 8: 19, 22–24).

Patient Endurance

There is such a future, or what I sometimes refer to as an eschatological dimension, to this Kenosis. What happens now has future hopeful dimensions. The fullness is somewhere in the future, and what we do now rushes us further into it. As St. Paul said to the Christian community in Rome:

> I consider the sufferings of the present time unworthy to be compared with the glory that one day will be revealed in us (*Romans* 8: 18).

Someone once said that God invented time because he didn't want everything to happen all at once! I believe this. But God also invented it so that all of us would be a part of shaping it and making it happen. He believes in us, and trusts us with this precious gift!

In order for me to be of any service to the Kingdom, I think I must realistically know myself, good and evil. I must reasonably accept, love, and believe in myself. Yet, I must continually run for the prize as creation waits and my own self inwardly groans with incompletion, for final glory, fulfillment, and redemption. By the Grace of God, I am on the way, but I also believe through that same Grace I have a good chance of coming to completion because of the Lord's Promise and Power!

CHAPTER 3

Community/Self Kenosis: Living

And the Lord gave me brothers.

—*Testament of St. Francis*

The friar's cell is his body . . .
his monastery . . . where his brothers are.

—*St. Francis*

Wherever the brothers meet, let them show that they are
members of the same family. And they should have no hesita-
tion in making known their needs to one another. For if a
mother loves and cares for her child in the flesh, a friar should
certainly love and care for his spiritual brother all the more
tenderly.

—O.F.M. Rule of 1223, *Omnibus*

Blessed is that servant who does not pride himself on the good
that the Lord says or does through him, anymore than on
what the Lord says or does through another.

—Admonitions XVII, *Francis and Clare*

An old man said: Do not despise your neighbor, for you do
not know whether the Spirit of God is in you, or in him.

—Nomura Yushi, *Desert Wisdom*

Blessed is the servant who would love his brother as much
when he is sick and cannot repay him, as he would when he is
well and can repay him.

—Admonitions XXIV, *Francis and Clare*

THE IGNACIO DE LA MANCHA STORY

Before ordination I had the wonderful opportunity to spend three summers working with migrant workers in southern New Jersey. One of the attractions of this ministry for me was that it drew enthusiastic, young, idealistic friars to it. We had the chance to live simply in a small community, in an old house in Elmer, New Jersey.

The diocesan priests in the neighboring parishes became our friends, for we used their churches for our masses and other services in Spanish. I could tell they kind of got a kick out of this poor band of friars in brown robes. They would often visit us for good times, prayer, and fraternity.

I remember one evening we friars joined about twenty priests at a celebration of the ending of forty-hours devotion. There were cocktails served after the closing and dinner to follow. Being out of practice from drinking I seemed to tip a few too many. After staying later with one of the friars, on the way home I lost my supper out of the window of the car, hoping the driving friar wouldn't notice. He didn't say anything.

I felt so ashamed. I got sick again when home. I was so sad and embarrassed, feeling I had let both my brothers and myself down. I just sat on my bed crying.

Iggy, now a missionary in Bolivia, came right over to me. I always looked up to Iggy. He challenged me because he took poverty and St. Francis so seriously. He was the first of us to work with the migrants.

Well, Iggy just put his arm around me, kind of rubbed my back, let me cry, and told me both he, the friars, and God still loved me. Iggy grew up in an alcoholic home and I'm sure he had seen this scenario before. Realizing that, and beginning to feel for him, and from him God's love, my tears turned from shame to a true humbling experience of joy at receiving this very free gift of unconditional love. Iggy's Kenosis revealed to me the marvelous merciful love of the Master and the joy of the prodigal son.

THEOLOGICAL DIMENSION OF COMMUNITY/ SELF KENOSIS

Being a friar, a little brother, a Franciscan is part of my interior life, part of my make-up as a person and minister. Because the brothers are not myself, but are outside of me, I not only receive from them the incentive to grow, but I must also reach out to them as others in service. And so, throughout this chapter, which is at the real working level of my daily life, I will consider both the influence my brothers have on my life, and also my service to them. This chapter will be a bridge between the first two chapters and the last. The first two considered my interior life, disposition, and attitudes as a minister, and the last looks at my ministry, performance, and service to the people.

Because of the vast influence community has on my life and ministry, this will be longer than the first two chapters. I will discuss the ordinary friars with whom I came in contact at St. Francis; the friars of my own peer group and status; and my supervisors, friars with whom I had this special helpful relationship.

To an age which glorifies and seeks individualism as a *modus agendi*, I believe that brotherhood and community are contradictory to twentieth-century America. Yes, there are trends that seem to be seeking community today. To me it seems that individualism, independence, isolation, and alienation, however, are the real-life situation of most modern Americans.

Franciscans seek to be a sign of the Church to the World, a working, throbbing, growing organ in the Body of Christ. Friars try to be witnesses to the possibility of nonalienation and brotherhood present in the Kingdom already at hand, and promised in the future Kingdom not yet present in its fullness.

An intricate part of my ministry to the world is helping to build up my own Franciscan fraternity to witness to the world of the presence of Christ's saving community, and the possibility of nonalienation. At the same time, there is a mutual exchange of love and *Diakonia* (service) going on within the brotherhood of friars, building up each other individually, and in turn, building up the fraternity.

How a minister is with God and with his own person cannot help but emerge in one's relationship and service to others. ''He who says he loves God, but hates his brother, is a liar" (1 *John* 4: 20). Jesus seemed to speak of how one's personal integration has an effect on others when he said: "The mouth speaks what the heart is full of" (*Luke* 6: 45). Being a member of community serves others, has an outward effect on the world, not only as a witness of the possibility of community, but being community is a way of service. Loving in a fraternity has helped me to be a more complete person, enabling me to serve better. Also, working as a team member with other friars has a great effect on the quality of my service to others. And so, we see how really all the first three Kenoses have an effect on how one serves, as will be discussed in chapter four, how one lives the Others/Self Kenosis.

To me, community exists where people seek to live what the Lord has commanded: "Love one another, as I have loved you" (*John* 13: 34). It exists where people seek "to lay down their lives for their friends" (*John* 15: 13). This laying down one's life is again the essence of the Kenosis called for in communal life. This Kenosis, as will be seen in the following pages, will take on many forms: listening to, growing together, suffering with, respecting, supporting, building up, praying with, being hospitable to, and most simply, "bearing with one another" (*Col.* 3: 13), all forms of communal life.

"Koinonia (Community) is a ministry and function of the Church, as is Kerigma (Proclamation of the Word), and Diakonia (Service)."[1] Koinonia in the Church is like the Eucharist. It both signifies unity and causes it. Koinonia, like the Eucharist, has both a present reality and an eschatological one, one pointing to the future possibility.

And so, every community finds its source in the Eucharist, which both signifies the community of faith that exists already, as well as causes further, deeper unity.

As the Church seeks to serve the World as community, so does every local Church or fraternity attempt to serve the world in which it finds itself. I will now try to share how I experience Kenosis within my community.

PERSONAL CHALLENGES AND LEARNING EXPERIENCES AT ST. FRANCIS

One of the greatest challenges for me was to live and work with an older community. Here was I, a young cleric, facing friars of all ages. My attitude, as well as the practical aspect of Kenosis here, was to tread lightly, not to bulldoze my "young liberal self" into their lives and their apostolate. My attitude was a kenotic one. I wanted to see, to respect, to learn from, to appreciate these older friars. I found three practical ways to experience Kenosis here: by listening, by being hospitable, by consoling.

Surprisingly, I found myself listening "therapeutically" in a brotherly way to older friars, who just needed to tell their age-old stories and history to someone. I found myself trying to be hospitable to visiting friars, trying to make them feel at home. I found myself attempting to console friars in need, or simply encouraging others when they needed it.

At St. Francis, the way priests celebrated Mass, the way the brother-in-charge ran the information desk, and the way things were done in general were constant challenges of adjustment for me. I waited always until I built up trust with other friars before I made suggestions to them. They did not have to do it my way!

Some friars were caught up in themselves and repeated old stories. Listening to them required my continual patience and kindness. They liked to pass on history.

A few friars were rehabilitating from alcoholism. I did my best to encourage and support these men, often going out of my way to do so. I also endeavored to learn about the disease.

Through our visitors, I truly experienced the catholicity of our order and church by living at St. Francis Friary. The friar who lived next door to me was Peruvian, studying English. He often stayed by himself during meals. I sat with him, exercised my Spanish, and urged him to speak more English. We both benefitted. A native Japanese friar was visiting from Tokyo. I went out with him, showed him New York City, and kept him company. Cardinal Antonelli brought many Third Order Franciscan women from Italy to New York City. They celebrated Mass in Italian, French, and Latin. Just seeing them gave me true insight into the universality of our Church.

One evening some friars and I enjoyed giving prayer support to a friar on the eve of his solemn vows.

A friar from one of our parishes was upset because another friar there was leaving the Order. I did my best to support this distressed friar, by just listening.

One incident helped me to experience supporting friars in another apostolate. Friars working with migrants in southern New Jersey asked me if I could meet a Puerto Rican migrant worker at Port Authority and place him on the Long Island railroad. Since I knew Spanish, I met this man in my religious habit at Port Authority and brought him to the Long Island railroad.

Areas of Resistance

Often I was bored with friars' old stories and stopped being present to them. At times, I purposely did not give older friars the attention they deserved by not asking them questions about their history. Otherwise they'd be off and running. Occasionally, I just gave up on the grouches who would never even say "hello" or respond to me.

Sometimes I think I may have overlooked too much when I saw that things were wrong. At times I found it difficult to know how and when to express confrontation or disagreement. I sought to prevent myself from mere reactions to friars, in favor of true charitable responses, but it wasn't always easy. I didn't always do it.

Ramifications for Ministry

Once again, I realized that God will not be outdone in generosity. In the Prayer of St. Francis for Peace it truly is in "giving that we receive." Often when I spent time speaking with an older friar, thinking I was a martyr, I was surprised all of a sudden to receive some huge insight from him.

I learned one evening after speaking and arguing with three older conservative friars that it is much more important to seek and celebrate those things that unite us, such as our faith and our life together, and especially that we are working for the same goals, rather than concerning ourselves with what divides us.

There was an older brother, Franky Schmitt, O.F.M., who was custodian of the dining room. His untiring labor was truly an inspiration to me. In him I saw simple faith in action without glamor and a demonstration of the Lord's words: "I am among you as one who serves" (*Luke* 22, 26).

I think that I should become more aware and conscious of time. Many friars with whom I lived have done so much to build up St. Francis Church and our Holy Name Province. I should become more acquainted with the past and present contributions of those friars in order to be challenged by their contributions to help mold our present and forge our future, perhaps refounding our Province with new vitality.

There will always be differences in personalities among people who live and work together. I should regard them not as threatening, but as enriching, so that together with these different personalities, using and employing our differences, we might become a better, more effective team and community.

Often we let little things bother us. I have learned to be more tolerant and to appreciate different ways of doing things. It is not worth the aggravation to quibble. This has taught me that things will work out even if they are not done my way.

Living with the friars at 31st Street, I have come to see something of what the words of St. Francis mean in the *Rule of 1223*:

> Wheresoever the brothers are and meet together, let them show that they are members of the same family, and frankly expose their needs to one another, for if a mother loves and cherishes the son that is born to her, how much more should one love and cherish his spiritual brother.

Through the different friars I lived with and met there, I came to be on both the giving and receiving end of those words, and that experience caused me once again to employ the words of the psalmist: "How good it is and how pleasant it is, where brothers live together as one" (*Psalms* 133: 1).

MY PEERS AT ST. FRANCIS

Now I will deal mainly with the three other young friars who were living and working with me at St. Francis. I will also mention other

people in different stages of development in their Franciscan vocation. I met and ministered to many of these people and so wanted
to include them here. These will include men who were friars in the
past and have left the Order; men who are presently in prenovi-
tiate formation; and young men who may be comtemplating a
future with us in the Order.

Competition

I found the chief dimension of Kenosis here to be personality
clashes and differences between myself and my peer groups. I
know that I have a strong personality that people usually cannot
react to with indifference.

I found there to be three chief dimensions of Kenosis here with
peers: understanding, accepting, bearing with.

Often I notice that my peers and I compete with each other. One
of us has outstanding qualities and subtly parades them, or looks
down on others who do not have them. Or, if we do not personally
possess certain qualities, we rip apart someone who does. The
Kenosis here seems to be to try to see the world from the other's
viewpoint and to try to understand him. After seeing the other
honestly, it appears that we must try to appreciate and accept that
brother the way he is and even encourage the differences.

Sometimes there is nothing glamorous, adventurous, or
dramatic about a relationship with another brother. However,
like another dimension, the constant challenge of Kenosis is to
"bear with one another" (*Col.* 3: 12), and at times just walk alongside or work alongside that brother in silence. Sometimes it's just
that!

Some Experiences

Daily: As a group of young friars, we looked out for each other.
For me it was always a special moment in a friary of over sixty
men to see one of these other young friars. To eat together, to
see each other at Divine Office, to relax in the evening in the
recreation room, these were all occasions I was especially happy
to share with Vinny and John.

Frequently we spontaneously shared with one another in supportive prayer. This demanded being aware of the other's moods and needs and being ready and prepared to pray with him. Sometimes our prayer was peaceful silence shared in the small chapel near my room.

One of our peers was a novice, out of novitiate on active apostolate for a month. We made an extra effort to watch out for him and to include him in things.

Weekly: We had different shifts on the information desk, preaching, and other duties, but one thing we all did together was to work every Thursday afternoon with the senior citizens. This was a ministry we all shared at the same time and enjoyed doing together.

Another activity we shared, which was a special moment of every week for me, was our weekly liturgy together with our supervisors. This was a time to relax together in the Lord's presence after a long day, a time to meditate on our past week's activities and ministry, and especially to give thanks for it.

Our weekly group discussion with our supervisors was another highlight of the week's activities. Our meetings usually consisted of discussing our homilies from the past week, both criticizing and being criticized, all in a positive manner. This was also a time to share reflections, both theological and practical, on aspects of our ministries. I didn't always look forward to going to these, but I always seemed to get something out of them.

Special Events: I once felt John was uptight from work and life in general at St. Francis, so I brought him home to my house on Long Island. We had a fine time.

We often spent our days off together, either going away somewhere or enjoying the city. One night we went to Coney Island, which was a thrill for us.

Past Vocations: New York City is central for many ex-friars, and St. Francis Church is well known to them. Often old friends (ex-friars) stopped in to visit. At times this was awkward, but I always tried to show interest and be encouraging. It wasn't something I always enjoyed. Their bitterness or their discomfort in their present lives is not always easy for me to handle.

Presently-in-formation: Often I feel that vocation directors break their backs to get men into our formation programs, and then seem to forget about them. I always tried to include and make our men in formation feel at home at St. Francis in whatever way I could. I often brought them down to the refectory to eat, or to the recreation room for a cold drink. Generally, whenever they were around, I tried to make them feel like real members of the fraternity.

Areas of Resistance

Often my expectations were too high. I expected unfairly from brothers what I ought only to expect from myself.

Sometimes I found myself trying to dominate a relationship by always keeping the control of it, by giving all the time instead of allowing the other person a chance to give. I tended to hide my needs from others at times rather than sharing them.

At times I noticed myself being stubborn, refusing to acknowledge the needs of a brother. If I saw someone hurting, I intentionally, out of selfish ambition, did not bother to minister to that brother.

I often found it difficult to be with ex-friars. Because of so many variables on both sides, it is hard not to make them feel excluded.

With young men in formation, at times, out of my own insecurity, I acted paternalistically to them.

When dealing with young men thinking of the friars, at times I was disrespectful of a person's own pace and time schedule. I must learn not to push a vocation, but to nourish it. I must always respect a person's freedom.

Ramifications for Ministry

I think I truly experienced with my peer group what team ministry means. We prayed, worked, recreated together. We criticized, challenged, and encouraged one another. "Where two or three were gathered in His name, there He was in our midst" (*Matt.* 18: 20). I experienced Church, fraternity, *Koinonia*, and ministry with these brothers.

We also shared *Kerigma* in that when any of us preached, others listened and helped the preacher grow with honest criticism and reaction. We also practiced *Diakonia*, by attempting to serve one another's needs.

The novice gave me great insight one evening in our group discussion. He talked about his inability to comfort and console his people in the hospital ministry, and how he was truly learning what it meant to pray the words "into your hands, O Lord, I commend my spirit," after he had done all he humanly could.

I was thrilled at the challenge offered to me by Rob, a young man searching for his vocation. He, in his own honest life quest, confronted me on my own level of values where I needed refreshment and renewal most.

One of the major lessons for me was that I have to learn to sense my own unfolding, as well as the development of my brothers. We must always give each other enough room to grow and to expand, by our understanding, acceptance, and our bearing with each other.

Professionally

A great deal of benefit comes from sharing experiences in a group. It allows one to compare, to test reactions, perhaps to role play, to enrich one's own pastoral skills by hearing how other men handle situations, and to understand what their attitudes are about certain concrete aspects of ministry. It is good to criticize constructively and be criticized. It is good for one's ego, as well as for one's ministry. I will try in any pastoral situation in my future to seek out a group like this. I found it helpful and necessary.

V. discussed a case of a parent worried about his son's possibly being a homosexual. V. treated the person rather than the problem, which we all agreed was the best procedure, especially without the son's being there. This was a good pastoral insight: the person is always more important than the problem.

R. also discussed ministry to dying people and how important nonverbal communication can be in ministry: being present in the room, a simple touch, holding someone's hand, having an understanding face. All these gestures communicate presence, care, and concern.

Encouraging One Another

> Let us be concerned with one another, to help one another to show love and to do good. Let us not give up the habit of meeting together, as some are doing. Instead, let us encourage one another, all the more since you see the Day of the Lord is coming near (*Heb.* 10: 24).

That verse and the following are my conclusion about my peer group:

> The group of believers was one in mind and heart. With great power the apostles gave witness of the resurrection of the Lord Jesus, and God poured rich blessings on them all. There was no one in the group who was in need. (*Acts* 4: 32–34).

I feel we were united in mind, heart, and spirit and that we shared all we had with each other.

PRACTICAL DIMENSION OF KENOSIS

Blaise Hamaday, O.F.M., was my general supervisor for all of my ministerial experience. I met with him once a week for at least one hour. John McVean, O.F.M. was my specific supervisor for the work with the senior citizens, as well as with the people of the Aberdeen Hotel. Fr. McVean was always at our group supervisory meetings and we met and spoke informally quite often.

The relationship with a supervisor was indeed an area of great potential for me. However, before this relationship could be beneficial, I had to do much dying to self and continue this throughout the experience. The practical tasks of this Kenosis dealt with the following: being afraid; admitting the need for a supervisor; being open and honest; making it work.

I had to overcome a fear I had of supervision before we could work well together. This was because, in my past, I had experienced an unpleasant counseling relationship with a spiritual director which I did not find to be beneficial.

I was afraid that this new relationship might not be successful. Therefore, I had to overcome my past fears, give it a chance, and be open to a new possibility.

Admitting again my limitedness and my need for a supervisor was another practical Kenosis I had to make. I had to admit that I didn't know all there was to know about ministry, and that someone else could actually help me grow and learn more.

To be open and honest was a constant challenge. I would have to be painfully truthful if I were to learn anything and grow from this supervision. Otherwise it would be a sham.

There had to be a constant effort to make it work. At each meeting I had to manifest my experiences, listen to Fr. Blaise, and be as completely present to our discussion as possible.

I will comment on my supervision experience on a threefold time line of: initial, process, termination.

Initial: Father Blaise took time out to give me a tour of the friary and church, pointing out everything of interest and importance. This impressed me favorably and made me feel welcome.

My first supervisory session was relaxed, yet efficient. We spoke about our mutual need to be open and honest, and that our sessions would be confidential. We discussed what I expected from a supervisor. I told him I was hoping that he would help me to reflect on my role as a minister, as well as my functioning in that role. I asked him if he would keep the theme of Kenosis in mind as a theological theme, in order to help me reflect on it and gain new insights into it based on my experience. This more or less concluded our contract of supervision.

Fr. Blaise told me he liked my first homily. We then discussed two cases I had encountered in counseling duty.

Process: Most of our sessions lasted well over an hour. Most of them dealt with cases I had in counseling, or with particular problems either Fr. Blaise or I was having with my ministry, or we discussed how I was feeling personally. A great part of my learning in the other areas of ministry flowed from my supervisory sessions with Fr. Blaise. The greatest attribute I could pay to him was that I think he honestly tried to serve me: coming to know me, challenging me, advising me, encouraging me even in things he himself would not choose to do. He truly was ''client-centered'' in the Rogerian sense. He truly tried to serve my needs as a young minister, and helped me mature.

Fr. Blaise had a great deal to offer. Having been at St. Francis for six years, in addition to his knowledge in the field of pastoral counseling, his experience made him well-equipped to be a supervisor. Fr. Blaise was sensitive, intelligent, critical, and most importantly, pastoral. He also was keenly aware of making me feel appreciated, both with regard to my talents and my performance. He gave me what was his to share, and also appreciated what insight I might have to give him. I felt that an openness and a mature respect always existed between us.

Fr. Blaise felt a desire to keep a professional distance between us when we weren't concerned with ministry, in order to maintain his mentor status as a service to me. I think that this was successful. Therefore, we recreated together occasionally, but not as a policy.

The process of our supervisory meetings dealt with two main areas: my apostolate or work; myself as minister.

My cases (for lack of a better word) were always discussed at our meetings. Theological difficulties I might be having, as well as any specific pastoral problems, were the content of our discussions.

One theological difficulty I had was people's devotion to the Blessed Mother, St. Anthony, and many other saints. I felt at times that the priorities of the people were misplaced. People thanked St. Anthony for favors instead of God. They walked around kissing statues in the church during Mass. There were many other pious practices.

I think that through this difficulty, and my discussions with Fr. Blaise, I came to a healthy appreciation of the Catholic theology of instrumentality, how the Lord works through humans, whether through his own Son Jesus, or through other people called saints, and that the Lord seems to work also through matter (sacramentals). Grace builds on and works through nature. This seemed very Catholic to me, and reminded me of the Catholic use of sacraments. In concrete ways, through concrete people, we can somehow come to experience God.

Saints seem to me to be different manifestations of different qualities of God. When people praise the saints, they are really praising God. Even though there truly are extremes in this regard, many people are led to God through the saints. It puzzles me why they can't praise God directly. However, as Fr. Blaise would say: "If it wasn't for St. Anthony, hundreds of people would not be coming to receive the Lord in the Eucharist every Tuesday."

Somehow in all of this I received a sense of traditional and, I think, pretty sound Catholic theology.

Another theological difficulty I had was the selling of Mass cards at the information desk. This was a constant preoccupation when working on the desk. People asked, "What can I get for $10.00?" or "How much are the Masses?" At times this disturbed me deeply. No one can buy a Mass!

Sometimes if I thought that the person was receptive to learning, I tried to explain that the offering was for the support of the friars (or for the materials used at Mass), and that all donations get the same benefits, except perhaps for the size or shape of the card.

I did come to a pastoral reason for Mass cards. It does make people feel good if they can have prayers (Masses) said for their loved ones. And it does seem to be a faith expression for those requesting the Masses as well as for the bereaved.

Fr. Blaise and I also discussed different reasons why people came to see a priest. Some had their minds made up and tested their position against yours; for example, one woman asked me the Church's views on astrology. One man, after having what he considered a religious experience induced by drugs, wanted to share it with a religious person. Some people are con artists, and all they are looking for is a handout.

We discussed how there is not always a give-and-take in ministry. Sometimes all you do in counseling is get psychologically drained, giving, ministering to people, but receiving nothing or very little in return.

Periodically, we discussed how I was feeling as a minister. For instance, we talked about the frustration of being available on counseling duty when no one comes for counseling. I could never really get involved with anything while on duty. When no one came, the day seemed just wasted.

We discussed my feeling a lack of accomplishment. Fr. Blaise always helped me to put this into perspective, considering the nature of the apostolate at St. Francis, and my short period of time spent there. This did not remove the feeling, but it was good to talk about it.

We discussed getting hurt when you go out of your way, laying down your life for another, and finding out that you risked in vain. One day I brought a young man down to Port Authority and bought him a ticket to Trenton. The con artist went to the bathroom and never got on the bus. And I never saw him again. Fr. Blaise knew how this hurt me. He helped me to bear it and laugh it off. "You win some, you lose some."

In general, Fr. Blaise was always around. If I needed to talk, needed advice, if I met a case too difficult to handle, he was always ready and willing to help.

Areas of Resistance

At times, I think we both resisted meeting together, by being late for our one-to-one hourly session every Wednesday afternoon. We sometimes either lacked agenda or enthusiasm.

At other times, I used defense mechanisms, giving in to the temptation to over-explain myself until he understood. Perhaps I feared challenge, critique, or confrontation. Sometimes, rather than listening and learning as he spoke, I would be preparing my next defense of why I did this or that.

And still on other occasions, you might say I was guilty of "pleasing the teacher." I did not challenge his viewpoints, either to stay on his good side or simply to avoid conflict. In general, however, especially with people I respect, like Fr. Blaise, I think I was honest.

Ramifications for Ministry

One evening during our group seminar, Fr. McVean led a discussion about the place of St. Francis Church in New York City, and what a minister can do. We considered some of the aspects of city life such as: speed, how city dwellers always seem to be trying to beat the clock; impersonalism, how the average city dweller or worker prefers to remain anonymous and perhaps lost in huge numbers of people; coldness, how people tend to deal with you efficiently and that's about it, showing very little personal interest.

Very generally, we mentioned how the Church, St. Francis Church, and ministers like ourselves can add some shade of meaning and personalism to the city by our treatment of the people who come to us. We can relay a certain stability, warmth, and peace to a city distraught by conflict, commotion, and confusion.

There is and always will be the need for people who exist purely as witnesses to God's presence by who they are and by their various services to people. Being the Church and realizing one's duty to represent the Kingdom of God is the continual and changing challenge of every minister.

As a future thrust, resulting from my limited experiences as preacher and counselor, I truly realized my desire for a fuller participation in ministry as a priest. I would like to lead communities in Eucharist, and to celebrate the life and presence of the Lord in the Sacraments for the Church. I also look forward to ministering the healing forgiveness of Christ in Confession, rather than having to refer people to another friar who is a priest.

Professionally

Fr. Blaise made me keenly aware of the reality of transference in counseling. People treat you, the counselor, as someone else whom you might remind them of, a parent, perhaps, or an old boyfriend. This is equally true for the counselor. He can experience the same thing toward the client. This is called countertransference.

Fr. Blaise always drummed into me the need to listen properly to people, not only to the words or content, but also to the feelings and nonverbal communication. Many times during our sessions, he interrupted my narration of a case and asked, "Now what do you really think that person is saying, Kevin?" He helped me to become a good listener.

My relationship with Fr. Blaise as my supervisor was indeed one of the highlights and most beneficial experiences of my ministerial experience.

There is only one suggestion that I would have offered to Fr. Blaise: that he become as proficient in theological and spiritual reflection as he is in pastoral counseling. I think I initiated the majority of the former.

Considering the anticipation with which I began this relationship, I think that the greatest compliment I could pay to Fr. Blaise is to say that I hope I never have to be a minister without having someone like him to bounce ideas off, to share, to reflect, to grow with, and to be supported by. The Lord gave me a great brother!

CHAPTER 4

Others/Self Kenosis: Serving

I am among you as one who serves.

—Jesus, *Luke* 22:27

Where I am, there also will my servant be.

—Jesus, *John* 12:26

Let the greatest among you be the servant of all.

—Jesus, *Luke* 22:26

As generous distributors of God's manifold grace, put your gifts at the service of one another, each in the measure you have received.

—Peter, 1 *Peter* 4:10

God forbid that I should glory save in the cross of our Lord Jesus Christ. Through it, I am crucified to the world, and the world is crucified to me.

—Paul, *Gal.* 6:14

It is quite the same for you who hear me. When you have done all that you have been commanded to do, say, ''We are useless servants. We have done no more than our duty.''

—Jesus, *Luke* 17:10

Let us begin again to serve the Lord, my brothers and sisters, for up to now we have done little or nothing.

—Francis, on deathbed 1 Celano, 103, *Omnibus*

IN THE FIELDS WITH GOD

After spending three summers ministering to migrant workers in southern New Jersey, I decided to really jump in and live with them in one of the camps for a week. I knew one of the crew leaders, Ralph, and his family. He and his sons joked with me saying, "You'll be sorry! You'll never last! You're even loco for trying this!" They signed me up. I went.

I wanted to be one of them. I did not advertise that I was a friar; nor did I attempt to preach to them that week. Not many of them knew I was a friar either. I only wanted to be with them, and experience what it was like to be a farm laborer.

I bunked in a room with a Puerto Rican friend, Victor, who agreed to do the week with me.

I never knew I had so many muscles! Every single one of them was used the first day. For eleven hours we bent down and picked squash along seemingly endless rows of prickly plants which lined the fields! We wore hot, sweaty rubber gloves all day, too.

The next day it was tomatoes. Same thing for ten hours. Then peaches. The other workers felt so at home with me, I think I learned every curse word in Spanish that week. They didn't know who I was, which made me feel good that my experiment was working. Vic kept the secret, too.

Two new young migrants bunked in our room on Thursday. Ralph told me to watch out for them, that he did not trust them. "Hide your money! Lock things up!" I ignored the advice and trusted.

Payday was Friday night. At $79.00 for thirty eight hours of the hardest work I had ever done! I was proud to earn that paycheck! I played pool with the guys that night and had a few *cervezas frias* with them. They drank like fish on Friday nights. Now I understood why.

Saturday after lunch, our two new roommates left the camp. Little did I know they would leave with my cash and camera! I only found this out when we got back to camp at 5 P.M.

"Anybody else but you Padre!" said the others who went into town angry, looking for the thieves. We found them, but there was no way of proving they had *my* money.

Upon returning to camp I had that lousy feeling of being robbed. I put my habit on for the first time and got ready to drive our bus to pick up people from other camps to bring to church. The men of the camp began coming to Ralph who was sitting across the table from me. One gave a twenty, another five, another ten, another three! What was going on? I said to Ralph, "This is not for me, is it? No, please don't!" They said: "Be quiet, Padre, we want to!"

I could not contain myself when Sam handed me the $105.00 these poor hard-working men collected! I felt so moved I could not speak! I could only cry! I felt so humbled, so accepted, so loved, so grateful to these men whom I had come to "pitch my tent among!"

Later that night, I asked some of the men in the bus why they did this. One of the older men put it all together for me: "Padre, cuando yo ando contigo en los campos, yo ando con Dios!" "Padre, when I walk with you in the fields I walk with God!"

I didn't think that they even noticed I was there! They experienced God walking in the fields that week, and believe me, so did I . . . one of the hundredfold in this life! To the praise and glory of God!

THEOLOGICAL DIMENSION OF THE OTHERS/ SELF KENOSIS

I will now focus on the essence of this reflection, the pastoral in-depth experience itself. The first three chapters were preliminary but essential considerations to what I am about to present. They studied the spiritual, personal, and communal character of the minister. All of these characteristics color how the minister will perform in ministry. That is why such time has been spent on the first three chapters. I invoke again the Latin expression: "action follows being." What one does in ministry will follow and flow from who one is as a person. That is why I have tried to present that person who is a minister in all the aspects through which his personality would influence his ministry.

The Kenosis for the God/Self was on a level of being; the Self/-Self on a level of believing; the Community/Self on a level of living; the Others/Self Kenosis on the level of serving.

As has already been stated, in order for one to give of oneself in loving service, one must be in touch with, and have a grasp of one's own self as a human being. In order to love others in service, there must be some preliminary love and acceptance of self. The Lord's command was "love your neighbor as you love yourself" *(Mark* 12:31). I think this implies that if we do not love ourselves, we aren't very likely to love others. Again, *Nemo dat quod non habet*. To the extent one loves self will one be able to love others. Quality of other-love is directly influenced by self-love.

All of Me

It seems to me that the minister is called to have his/her spiritual, theological, emotional, professional, human self all at the disposal of the People of God. The whole self must be available, when needed, and as much as is needed. The words of the Lord, "where I am, there also will my servant be" *(John* 12:26), imply that the Servant of God, in self-emptying, is to be wherever the Lord calls him/her to be, and is to be ready to give at that call whatever s/he has, according to the need of the other.

Jesus, at his Last Supper, displayed himself as a Servant, especially through his Word and Action in the Gospel of St. John. "But if I washed your feet—I who am Teacher and Lord, then you too must wash each other's feet" *(John* 13:14). It seems to me that the follower of Jesus, the minister, must see her/himself as servant of all.

Along with Eugene Maly, I see the ministerial notion of Servant in two general ways.[1] One way is a general type of service doing various works for people: "feeding the hungry"; "preaching when convenient and inconvenient, instructing, rebuking"; encouraging, "building up the body"; "being with" people, being "Greek with the Greeks, and Jewish with the Jews, all things for all people in order to save a few" (1 *Cor.* 10, 31–33).

The second way of service is an Old Testament Biblical notion referring to the Suffering Servant of Yahweh of *Isaiah* 53, who suffered and offered his life vicariously for others. 'Greater love than this no man has that he lay down his life for his friends" *(John* 15: 12–13). This suffering is redemptive for it brings about change, new life. Modeling ourselves after the great Servant Jesus, the eternal High Minister Jesus, "by whose wounds we were healed" *(Isaiah* 53, 5), St. Paul urges his fellow Christians to make up for what is lacking in the sufferings of Christ *(Col.* 1:24), reminding us of our part in redemptive suffering for the Body of Christ, already perfect, yet still growing to full maturity.

My understanding of the above is that to empty myself in service to others, in so many general ways, as well as at times to suffer vicariously for others, is to help bring about the redemptive new life of Jesus Christ in the lives of his people, and is a way of helping others to realize the Good News in their existential lives.

Serving, Proclaiming, Forming Community

As the Church is the Servant of the World, the minister is the servant of the Church. And as the Church has the threefold function of *Diakonia, Kerigma, Koinonia* for the world,[2] so does the priest have this same threefold ministry to the Church: of serving the Kingdom (Diakonia), proclaiming its presence (Kerigma), and forming it in the people, building community (Koinonia).

Diakonia (service) is the principal theme of this chapter. Each of these three functions overlaps in my understanding. Diakonia consists of proclaiming the Word, and forming Christian Community. Kerigma consists of living the Word in service and in becoming community. Koinonia is proclaimed in the Word of the Lord, and expressed in the service of charitable deeds. As the Church must work (serve) to bring about God's Kingdom, so must she be a symbol of it (community) as well as proclaim it (word). As the Church is for the world, the minister must be the servant of, the symbol of, the Word made flesh of—the reality of God's Presence —the Kingdom.

In all these functions, the Church and minister proclaim present realities and yet future fulfillments, the Kingdom's presence at hand and yet the future Kingdom where peace and justice will reign "where every tear shall be wiped away" *(Rev. 21:4)*.

The minister attempts to minister reconciliation and healing by serving, preaching, and forming of community. At times this service, proclamation, or celebration of community will be expressed or celebrated sacramentally.

With service as the chief orientation of this chapter, I will deal with the kenotic experiences which the minister undergoes who dares to serve others, who dares to attempt to walk in the footsteps of the Master, who "emptied himself" totally, "unto death on the cross" *(Phil.* 2:8).

This service, this emptying is not done for one's own sake, but is done, whatever its manifestation, for the sake of hoping to form the unity of all humankind as brothers and sisters in Jesus Christ as adopted sons and daughters of the one Holy God. This self-gift is offered freely by the minister in the hope that in his self-emptying in love, the presence of the Lord and his saving grace will be felt by the individual receiver, by the Church, and ultimately by the world:

> so that all may believe that He has been sent by the Father, so all may be one, even as you, Father, are in me, and I am in them, so that they may be one in us *(John* 17:21).

One ultimate aim of ministry is the unity and reconciliation of people to people, and all people to God.

> The minister, according to the recent theological study of the priesthood commissioned by the bishops of America, is to be the "sign and agent of reconciliation."[3]

PRACTICAL DIMENSION OF OTHERS/SELF KENOSIS

In order for one to preach the Lord's Word and not one's own, one must be in constant communication through prayer with the Lord. One must also be deeply in touch with one's own feelings and moods, so as to realize how to purify oneself in preaching the Lord's Word. Also, if one is to be prepared satisfactorily, one must spend adequate time studying the readings, thinking, praying, writing, rethinking, and rewriting one's homily. A spirit of prayer, freedom from selfishness, and adequate preparation all seem to be part of the Kenosis called for in the service of preaching God's Word.

Not only is one to take oneself into consideration, but also the audience to whom one is preaching. How to speak the Lord's Word, expressing both comfort and challenge, is a constant task to be reckoned with. One can easily preach a watered-down message, which would not bother anyone. Or, one can preach hellfire and brimstone. I think that Kenosis demands one to preach the Word as one feels, while adequately dealing with the two-edged nature of that Word: its love and its justice. I have always found Jesus to be the excellent model for this balance when He says to us: "Come to me all you who are weary and find life burdensome, and I will refresh you" (*Matt.* 11:28). He also says in the very same breath: "Learn from me" (*Matt.* 11:29). He comforts, accepts, welcomes us as we are; but also admonishes, confronts, and challenges us to become all that we can be. Preachers must do the same!

It is also important to take into consideration the makeup of the community. The challenge, as I see it, is to be as broad as possible because of the variety of people concerned, and yet to be as personal as possible in order to touch individuals.

Similar dimensions must be taken into account when one is exercising one's ministry as acolyte and in leading liturgical singing. I needed to be prayerful and devout, and at peace in myself. I had to prepare myself adequately, so as to modify my behavior according to the needs of the people, whether distributing Communion or leading liturgical song.

Examples from 31st Street

I had the opportunity of preaching at least once or twice per week. As has been mentioned already, I felt warmly received by the people, by their attention during the homilies and by their positive responses and compliments. The friars spoke positively about my preaching, also. Fr. Cosmis, the pastor, at whose Mass I regularly led the congregation in singing, was quite pleased with their participation because of me.

Even though my singing voice is not great, I felt that I encouraged the people to sing because I admitted to them what a terrible voice I had. In admitting my limits and weakness to them, it seemed they became animated to sing and to learn new songs.

Occasionally, I read a meditation prayer after Communion. More than once someone complimented me for this and asked for a copy of the prayer.

I especially enjoyed distributing Holy Communion. The devotion of the people was often impressive. At times, however, I did feel that their sacramental lives were isolated and separated from the rest of their lives. I noticed this at the kiss of peace—how cold it often was. But this is New York City, I reminded myself; I could not expect too much more. Considering the makeup of the congregations, as a community they did fairly well.

Giving the Bread of Life to people I had come to know and love during the summer was particularly enjoyable.

Areas of Resistance

There were, however, some areas where I was not emptying myself completely, and these areas could be continually problematic in ministry.

I think for a while during the summer I was disturbed, even depressed about the makeup of the clientele at St. Francis. I was young, long-haired, bearded, and I was hoping to work in some way with other young people. However, one of the reasons I went to St. Francis was to work with adults. I did not enjoy the absence of youth either in the Church during homilies, or on the Communion lines. When I did spot a youth, I geared my attention to him or her in a homily, or gave a little extra, or was more personal in saying "The Body of Christ, my friend," or something like that. I found this to be an ongoing concern of mine, one of which I had to be careful.

However, I do think that I handled this reasonably well. I began to appreciate more and more the adult community, and to my knowledge I did not alienate any older person through my own fault. I think it could be said that I served them maturely and adequately, and those who received my service seemed to appreciate it.

There was always a danger of not being prayerful or prepared for preaching, of just rambling on instead of being well-prepared and knowing what to say. However, I spent from three to five hours in prayer and preparation for each homily. I am grateful to God's Grace that preaching seems to be one of my strengths.

Another potential danger was trying to be too pastoral, not including new theology but resorting merely to traditional piety rather than challenging the people with new ideas and myself with creative pastoral ways of communicating these ideas. However, I believe this was more of a potential resistance than an actual one. I think my homilies were theological in content and appropriate.

On days when I was assigned to help distribute Communion at three or four Masses, there would be the possible resistance of becoming too robot-like, becoming mechanical or functional, rather than sacred and personal. This is a potential danger for me. The novelty and privilege of being an extraordinary minister of the Eucharist that summer never wore off for me.

There was another difficulty which I could have given into, but did not. Adequate communal preparation in song before the Eucharist was often trying and it was tempting to give up on it. This was so because the congregation varied from week to week; and therefore, no matter what songs I wanted to teach, they were always new to the people. The real trial was that most people came in to Mass only a few minutes before it started, and there was always pressure from priests and ushers to start on time. Because of the limits of what we could do, I could have given up, but I did not. I often compromised by teaching simple songs, or acclamations, which demanded very little practice.

An attitude that I constantly had to fight was not to give up on the people, to keep believing in them, that they wanted to learn new songs and to participate.

Ramifications for Ministry

In distributing Holy Communions and in preaching the Holy Gospel, I was challenged to love all of these people in some real Christian way, or the ministry for me would have been meaningless. I was reminded of the expansive and universal love the Lord has for all and each of his people, and that He is willing to offer himself daily to whoever wants to receive him, both in Word and in Sacrament.

Even if I speak with human tongues and angelic as well, but if I do not have love, I am a noisy gong, or a clanging symbol (1 *Cor.* 13:11).

I found that if I am going to do the ministry of the Lord, I must truly be willing to unite myself with Him, and say to his people with Him: "This is my Body, which will be given up for you" (*Luke* 22:19). Someday, I will say these words as a priest, and effect sacramentally what they signify. I must more and more unite myself with the Lord and try to love these people as he does, and continue to love them, even though they may not be personally appealing to me.

Building a liturgical Eucharistic community (Koinonia) at St. Francis is indeed difficult, especially if one is not a celebrant at the Mass. I do believe that something is happening there to the lives of the people involved, but often there are no real communal celebrations. Many of the people just come, pray, and leave that church as individuals, "me and God."

To my delight, I discovered that an aged body is not always indicative of an old heart. Many, many old people I found were indeed childlike in the way that the Lord speaks of childlikeness as a prerequisite for the Kingdom. Just as the elderly people had to get beyond my externals to me and the truth I had to share with them, so did I have to remove my prejudices and see these people without reference to their age.

I found a few ramifications for the ministry at St. Francis. Many of the friars did not seem to take the Liturgy of the Word seriously. They often zipped through it. No wonder Catholics have very little interest in the Bible. I would recommend that some of the friars stationed there be given some workshop on preaching and the Word of God.

I would have to make that a general recommendation also for the sacraments of the Eucharist and Penance. Because of the nature of St. Francis as a "service church" as earlier described, I feel it is imperative that such a sacramentally oriented church celebrate well and be an extremely good example for the whole of New York.

I do feel, however, that the friars there constantly seek improvement in their ministry.

Professional Growth

I learned to be more confident in public with people of all ages. I should fear nothing and no one so long as I am preaching the truth of the Gospel with love.

I also learned that occasionally it helps to expose one's own weakness, in order to motivate people to do things. This is a theme of the book, *The Wounded Healer*. I exposed some of my limitations and humanity to the people when leading them in singing. I challenged them by my "wounds," saying "If a voice like mine can dare to come up here and lead the singing at this microphone, none of you has any reason in the world to be ashamed of your own voice."

> Making one's own wounds a source of healing requires a constant willingness to see one's own pain and suffering (I would say limitation and humanity here) as rising from the depth of the human condition which all people share.[4]

This attitude is one I try to have in all of ministry, being a human among other humans, seeking transcendence with them.

Learnings for Future

Through my limited participation in the Sacramental ministry at St. Francis Church, I came to see just how important good preaching and good, lively, prayerfully well-planned liturgies are for building up the community. I became acutely aware of the importance of Liturgy of Word and Eucharist in the life of the Church. It is indeed a real privilege to serve the community in this way. It does demand much; but for the person of faith who believes in Him who will bless what the minister sows and reaps, it is well worth it, and worth preparing in every way for that ministry.

I also came to understand the words of Paul when he wrote to Timothy: "Do not let anyone look down on you, because you are young" (1 *Tim.* 4:12). For the most part, at this stage of ministry, I thank God that I do feel comfortable as a public minister of the Church. I became encouraged to see that I am fruitful and relatively at ease. I have also felt accepted in this role, and warmly received for the most part.

From this limited experience of formal church ministry, I feel comfortable looking forward to priesthood as a way that I can truly become more and more my full human self, that which the Lord created me to be, for the sake of others, for my happiness, and for his glory.

INFORMAL MINISTRY

Since the majority of my ministry was of this nature, this section will be more lengthy. I use the term informal in contrast to formal. Perhaps "unordained" ministry might be as good a title. I do not consider informal ministry as less genuine or less important than sacramental formal ministry. The informal ministry which I was engaged in at St. Francis consisted in the following: counseling, working on the information desk, distributing food on the morning breadline, meeting weekly with senior citizens, visiting the people of the Aberdeen Hotel one morning a week.

I have already discussed the general theological dimensions of the Kenosis of serving and so I will deal now with the practical dimension of the Other/Self Kenosis involved in serving people in informal ministry.

In order to describe the pastoral experience as well as analyze it (Areas of Resistance), I will deal briefly with each individual service: counseling, desk, etc. I feel that this is essential in order to show both the variety of the pastoral experience, and the depth of my pastoral reflection about the experience.

A great deal of my growth and learning during this summer originated in this area of ministry. This area was more often than not the topic for our supervisory sessions.

It is my opinion that much of the kenotic experience with others has to do with the ambiguity and limitations of the human being and the human situation. This complication of the human being becomes more complex when two people try to relate to one another. The minister loves and serves others in this situation. I believe that there are many dimensions of this Kenosis for the minister within this human condition.

Some dimensions of the Kenosis involved the following concerns: freedom, mutuality, receiving, listening, suffering, feeling with and for people, risking.

Freedom

A basic Kenosis is allowing other people to have their freedom. When the minister is trying to help someone, it is often difficult for the minister to wait until the person is ready to receive what the minister has to give. This is why in counseling, trusting relationships have to be built. The counselor must respect the stage where a person is. One is not permitted to bombard or smother the receiver with either more love, advice, or knowledge than the person needs or is capable of handling at one particular time. I believe that the Lord never forces his love on anyone, but his presence is there, available, ready to give as the receiver is ready to receive. "The Lord stands at the door knocking" (*Rev.* 3:20), waiting for us to open the door freely from inside, ready to receive what he has to give us. As the Lord respects our freedom, so the minister must die to self to truly be sensitive to what the other needs, and what the other can accept at a particular time.

Mutuality

Another area of ambiguity in serving others is the mutuality of the love exchanged. The minister is there to serve, 'to give freely to others, what he has freely received'' (*Matt.* 10:8). He must not look for recompense or for his ego to be built up. He is a servant of the Lord. He is not to work for his own needs to be fulfilled in the people to whom he ministers. His personal needs should be reasonably well taken care of in his personal life. Self-seeking in ministry is the exact opposite of self-emptying. If there is love returned, the minister should humbly accept it. This, however, should not be his/her motive. The ministry is not where one seeks his/her life, but where one loses it for others. In my experience, many clergy either consciously or unconsciously use ministry for their own ego-building.

Humbling

When a ministerial relationship does become mutual to some extent, this can be kenotic also. Receiving faith and love back from people we serve can be beautiful, but it also can be very humbling. I personally believe that this can be even more difficult, more self-emptying, and perhaps even more redemptive for others than giving them faith or love. Evoking, calling forth charity from others, is often much more challenging than bringing it to them.

Others feel worthwhile when they can give something. And so sometimes I believe it can be "more blessed to receive than to give."

On the other hand, there are relationships in ministry which would never be reciprocal. These are difficult and a perplexing question of Kenosis. Should one keep trying? How long must one love while nothing is returned? This is a dimension of Kenosis which to me seems to have no definite clear-cut answer, and continually remains a problem in ministry.

Listening

Another practical dimension of Kenosis in serving others is knowing that much of one's service to people will imply a certain form of presence, for instance, listening. Listening to people, rather than giving them answers, can be draining. But since life's problems are frequently complex, and many difficulties are unsolvable, the minister is often called to be with someone simply as a listener, to enable that person to ventilate, to tell a sad or happy story. I think that it is even a further development of this Kenosis to continue to enter into situations like this, knowing that one will probably be unable to solve a particular problem. Obviously, this can be frustrating. It would be much easier to avoid situations when I know I can't really affect a change. Being helpless here is kenotic.

It is comforting to know, however, that people often realize the minister cannot solve their problems, and finding someone who will listen was really all they were looking for anyway. Just listening can be redemptive, because it saves the person from being alone. Becoming a good listener can be a life-long task. It is an active engagement; one is not merely a passive sponge receiving. Very few people do it well. I believe we are meant to do twice as much listening as talking. After all, God gave us all two ears, but only one mouth! "Listen that you may have life" (*Isaiah* 55:3).

Suffering

Another dimension of Kenosis, closely related to listening, from the vantage point of the minister, is suffering, i.e., letting others suffer. Often one has to stand by, stand near and watch others suffer, whether it be mental illness, (at the Aberdeen Hotel), loneliness (derelicts and alcoholics on the breadline), or physical death (senior citizens). It is tempting to hide from situations of suffering like this and not enter into them, or to deny that suffering exists when one is there in the situation. I think that Kenosis implies "being with" others in their suffering, allowing them to have it, not denying it. It is theirs. Sometimes suffering is all a human may have as one's own. Sometimes it can be all that someone is capable of or willing to share with others. If a minister denies the suffering of the person, he might be denying the person or cutting off a possible relationship.

It seems to me that the minister must try to help the person alleviate as much suffering as possible, but then also remain with the person while the ongoing, unrelieved suffering endures, at least so that s/he will not feel alone. Once again, this may not be physical healing or problem solving, but can be a redemptive presence to another, if the minister is willing to "pitch his tent" (*John* 1:14) among the poor, the suffering, the needy. Jesus did not walk around handing out dollar bills, or healing everyone in sight. I prefer to think of him in his redemptive, healing presence as "Emmanuel . . . God with us."

I believe what the minister does with the sufferings that s/he has to bear with others is also significant. I found that I could only bear them because I knew I could give them back to the Lord in prayer, for he bore all our sufferings and conquered them. I took great consolation in knowing that I did not bear them alone for people, but that the Lord himself was yoked with me, the strong one continually giving me his support and his consoling words:

> Come to me all you who are overburdened and heavy-laden, and I will give you rest. Take my yoke upon you. (*Matt.* 11: 28–30).

Often Christians see their faith as a burden, being yoked with Jesus as a burden. I recently learned this meaning.

Our Franciscan missionaries in Brazil often have to go into the jungle during the rainy season when everything gets difficult because of the mud. Jeeps become stuck. The only way out of the mud is to get a big ox to pull the jeep out. Oxen know how to do the "ox thing." They are strong, and they just walk and pull. Little oxen learn how to be big, strong oxen by being yoked with a big, strong, more experienced ox. The little ox wants to run free, kicking and stretching. The tiny ox doesn't carry the load at all. Being yoked with the older ox, it learns to do the "ox thing," not really bearing any burden at all. Jesus carries us when we belong to him. We are yoked with him as learners, disciples.

Better than Others

A block to Kenosis I had to overcome was the illusion that I was better than the derelicts on the breadline or the poor at the information desk. Feelings of self-righteousness and self-achievement in comparison to others is anything but kenotic. To not look down on others, to not be paternalistic toward them was the constant challenge. I had to continually remind myself of my brotherhood and equality with them in my poverty of spirit before God and before other people.

Feeling overly pitying of these poor, I felt, was not kenotic either. Redemptive feelings for others will challenge them to come from their grim situations if possible. Pity tends to allow people to wallow in these situations without much hope.

Trying to figure out how to best deal responsively, respectfully, and redemptively with the poor is indeed a dimension of this Kenosis of service. There is always a risk, especially if the poor ask for money. There seems to be constant risk in listening to their stories or trusting them. It often seems to no avail. The minister can adopt two extremes—never to give, or always to give. It seems that a true Kenosis falls somewhere in the middle where responsibility and prudence exist.

Too often a minister might stop respecting these poor, whether they are derelicts or senior citizens. I felt a constant challenge to put myself in their shoes. At times I know I developed a terrible impersonalism towards the elderly senior citizens. Many had become hard New Yorkers with tough fronts that were difficult to break through or relate to. I was often reminded by them of the respect I need to pay to each individual. Paul mentions what I consider to be a good attitude here:

Do not rebuke an elderly man, but exhort him as you would a father, and young men as brothers, elderly women as mothers, younger women as sisters in all chastity. (1 *Tim.* 5 :1-2).

Allowing others their personal freedom to respond, not being self-seeking, appreciating the mutuality or nonmutuality of ministerial relationships, receiving love in humility, listening to others rather than solving problems, suffering with others, allowing them their personal dignity to suffer, respecting the poor as humans with worth, and serving the poor with responsibility were all practical dimensions of the Others/Self Kenosis as I experienced it in these informal, non-church ministries.

PARLOR DUTY EXPERIENCES

Counseling consisted of being assigned with Fr. Blaise from 2:00 P.M. to 8:00 P.M., being available to talk with anyone either in person or on the phone. The people usually asked for a priest. I always clarified that I was not a priest before I talked with them, in case they were planning on confession or explicitly needed a priest. No one ever refused to speak to me because I was not a priest.

Initially, I was filled with great anticipation, not knowing what people would want, need, or expect from me as a counselor. I wondered if I would be competent and capable of helping them. But after speaking with Fr. Blaise, I was relieved and less anxious. I found that "parlor duty" as we called this time, dealt with three general areas of concern: moral problems, spiritual problems, general help. I would like to present some examples from each area to give an idea of the counseling experience.

Moral Problems

Mr. P., forty years old, was having a drinking problem. Because of pressure from his wife, he wanted to take the sobriety pledge and get a blessing from the Church. He said he had done this before and it helped.

Instead of instantly letting him take the pledge, I talked with him a while about his problem. I asked him if he ever considered

Alcoholics Anonymous. The value of A.A. is that a person is not alone in his struggle for sobriety. After speaking for about a half-hour, I told him I would let him take the pledge if he promised to attend at least two A.A. meetings within the month. He said he would. I invited him to come back after about a month to let me know how he was doing. He never came. I thought it was a good session though. I hope he went to the meetings and was not just fooling both me and himself.

Mr. E. was forty-eight years old, and very anxious while speaking. He had just had a vasectomy and was wondering if he was excommunicated. When I didn't panic or appear shocked, he seemed to calm down a bit. I tried to explore why he had this done. He and his wife practiced rhythm for twenty-three years. They presently had three children, the youngest being eleven. The wife was nervous lately, had missed her period last month, and was terribly anxious about being pregnant again. Having an eleven-year-old when she was fifty-nine terrified her. He and his wife then looked into birth control pills. Unsatisfied with these, he decided for her sake to have a vasectomy.

He was terribly guilt-ridden about it. I tried to listen, and tried to help him see his problem within the perspective of their whole marriage. It was sinful because they thought it was. However, I did try to relate to him that it was not the end of the world, and perhaps it might have been the best thing for them to do in their situation.

Spiritual Problems

I saw nineteen-year-old Andi two or three times. She was Jewish and interested in Christianity. We discussed Jesus and the Christian faith, and also prayed. She and some of her friends at college were trying to live Christian lives. I tried to encourage her growth and faith, as well as give her some didactic input into the faith through our discussions.

Victoria was a forty-five-year-old school teacher in Harlem. She began our session by asking me what I thought of astrology. She had recently gotten involved with it, and was wondering what the Church taught about it. I spoke about it in terms of the power these things can have over our lives if we place too much emphasis on them, how we can eventually lose control of our lives, how we can lose our freedom. One might say it is almost like worshipping false gods. We talked for a while, then got into other topics, her faith being one of them. She felt she was growing weaker in her faith. After praying with her I suggested that she come to a prayer meeting with me. She came to two or three; we talked about her faith, life, etc. She grew, and we became good friends.

General Help

Ethel was sixty-eight, and a lonely old maid. She was currently having difficulties with her sister who was a grandmother with a large family. Ethel felt that her sister was ignoring her. We discussed the situation for a while, and she had a good cry for herself. Her tears arose from her nervousness as well as from her relationship problems. I was more a listener than anything else. I challenged Ethel, though, about her selfishness in their relationship. We ended with a prayer asking the Lord to bless her and her sister. She wrote me a week later, thanked me, and sent me $2.00.

Mrs. B. was a thirty-seven-year-old Haitian concerned about her husband's gambling. I tried to allow her to ventilate her feelings because I sensed real frustration in her. She seemed very concerned about solving this problem and I sensed her impatience. I excused myself from her to see if we had any referral agencies in our card catalog. I found *Gamblers Anonymous* and called them immediately. The man at the other end told me that this was the greatest telephone call I had ever made. He urged me to put Mrs. B. on the phone, but I didn't know if she was ready for something like this or not. I told her about this organization modeled after A.A. and urged her to try it. She seemed grateful that I had some alternative and said she would call them.

Anonymous Phone Calls

Often we got phone calls while on parlor duty from people who asked questions such as: "When does the Portiuncula indulgence become applicable?" or "What is the current Eucharistic fast?" or

"What is the Church's present teaching on . . .?" Even though these questions were relatively simple to handle, at times they were frustrating. Although one would like perhaps to educate people when they ask these questions, often all they want is quick information. Therefore, that is what should be given them, and was what I tried to give them.

Many sorts of lonely or seriously disturbed people called just to talk with someone. It was frustrating, not knowing the best way to help these people. Do we feed or help their neurosis by listening? What to do?

Mr. H. called and told me he was often very nervous at work. In his twenties, he told me that the men at work sometimes called him a homosexual, and sometimes this bothered him and made him wonder. After discussing this with him for at least fifteen minutes, I asked him if he would like to discuss sexuality with someone more competent and more familiar with these problems than myself. He quickly said, "I'm not a homosexual, Father." I found for him another friar who works with people having difficulties with their sexuality, and he made an appointment to see the friar.

The Front Desk

At the information desk I got another lively sense of the people who come to St. Francis. It was there also where for twelve hours per week, usually in two- or three-hour shifts, that I learned how important are the little sensitivities of ministry: a kind word, an understanding grasp of a bereaved person's hand, a warm smile, a Franciscan manner of being with people.

The other friars and I often reflected on the value of the "desk" for the friary. It was here that New Yorkers could see if friars are true Christians who have broken from the "rat-race" of the big city. Here in this business situation, would they be treated with personalism and kindness, or would they receive the cold efficiency of a bank teller, or the matter-of-factness of a store clerk from Gimbel's? People of all religious faiths come in touch with a representative of the friars, of the Catholic Church here at the desk. Although this job assignment may have seemed mechanical or unimportant, in the total ministry at St. Francis we saw it as vital and critical. It was here that many people received a prelude to how they would be treated either in confession or in counseling.

Businesspeople, secretaries, religious Sisters, workers, shoppers, all sorts of people came in and requested Mass cards, either for themselves or for others. Many of these people have been coming to St. Francis for years. They knew the friars and what to expect from them. I tried to give them nothing less.

Many Sisters and other people came in regularly to acquire Mass cards for the people they served. I used to make it my business to try to get to know these regular people and to encourage them in their work (many of these Sisters worked with the aging), and to try and express interest in their work and in them.

One day, I could see that a woman was upset about the loss of a dear one. She began crying as she was giving me the necessary information. It was awkward. I reached for her hand and held it. I could feel the strength going through me to her. She uttered a sigh of relief.

Often people brought religious articles to the desk to be blessed. I gave them to a priest and he blessed them for the people. When I brought them back, I said something like: "May this always remind you of how much the Lord loves you." Not being an ordained priest I could not bless things technically; but I often tried to say some words of blessing or to add my "two cents," for whatever it was worth.

Many of these people seemed to place much devotion in material things. One day a woman told me it was her forty-eighth wedding anniversary and that it would mean much for her if I could get a candle for her and place it before the altar of the Sacred Heart. I told her that I usually would not leave the desk but that she was special today. It is difficult to believe how much this meant to her. The candles had been sold out, but I acquired one for her.

Mass Cards

As previously mentioned, a most difficult problem for me working on the desk was the Mass cards, and having Masses said for people. I felt like a "buyer or seller in the temple". Often the people who requested the Masses seemed very superstitious. The more Masses they could have said, the quicker the soul would get to heaven. Also, another problem for me was their attitude of buying

Masses as if they were merchandise in a store. These attitudes were betrayed by phrases such as "What can I get for $10.00?" or "How much are the Masses?" While working through the theological issue in my head, I tried to keep myself grounded in pastoral concern, and tried to educate them by saying "There is a $2, $5, $10 offering, but a Mass is a Mass; the only difference is how much of an offering you would like to make." A Mass is of infinite value and really could never be purchased! I always got a kick out of people buying two or three "Perpetual Enrollments." How much more can you get than perpetual? But I was also grounded in the reality that our formation program in our province is supported by these offerings. Why not make this offering to the Church rather than some secular card store or florist? I do believe in our Church and it does need to be supported.

It troubled me also to see very poor, old women offering their last pennies to have a Mass said in honor of St. Anthony or for the poor souls, or in thanksgiving. At times like that I felt I was like Jesus witnessing the offering of the widow's mite. The simple faith of these little ones often put to shame my theological learning! They define theology as "faith seeking understanding." Often in theology class, I noticed much learning but frightfully little faith. I only wish I could supplement these people's faith with a bit more learning.

Handouts

There were also unfortunates who came asking for "carfare to Brooklyn" or a "dime for a cup of coffee." We were allowed to give out up to $5.00, depending on our own judgment. Usually we would give some change or a dollar or two depending on circumstances. The peculiar thing one learns after having been on the desk for two weeks or so is that when the "knights of the road" know that the new young friars are stationed at the desk and will be there all summer, they try to get whatever they can from us. Their most skillfully convincing tales suddenly surface to the forefront of their memories. You can be sure we heard their most successful, heart-rending stories, which were tried out again and again on each new batch of soft-hearted, naive friars. The word always got out when there was a "new kid on the block!"

The "regulars" are people who come at least two or three times a week, asking for money or clothes. Often we know what they will do with this money: buy themselves a bottle. It is really a dilemma. One does not know what will best help them. Are we fostering their dependence and/or immaturity by giving them money? This was the topic of many discussions among the friars. Each friar had to decide upon his own policy for himself. For me it is easy just to give a dollar. It is hard to try to communicate something to the men. Is this my cop out?

One day I tried to challenge one of these men. I said, "Mr. T., you don't have to live this way! Tell me about your life." He told me about it. I said, "I know you can get a job. You're different from the others who come in here. You have class!" He did wind up getting a job. Then, he worked on and off. But whenever I saw him on the street or the breadline, it became embarrassing. He told me, "I'm doing it for you, Brother Kevin, because you had confidence in me." He did seem to be doing well. That was a risk well-taken and worthwhile.

We had other characters come in, too. The friars seem to have a certain magnetic appeal. One rather large woman was always dirty, so much so that I never knew if she was black or white. She came in wearing fishnet sweaters with nothing underneath, asking for clothes, or with her potbelly hanging out. Despite her appearance, she was so sweet. We either gave her something, usually clothing (which we think she sold), or some small amount of money. Once I yelled at her for coming into the friary two weeks ago so indecently attired. She kind of chuckled, saying she was probably drunk at the time. I told her either to get a shower with this quarter, or never to come back! She stayed away for a while, but she always returned, usually unshowered.

After she'd been coming to 31st Street for years, we finally asked her name. It was Elizabeth. Somehow, and I'll never know why, we nicknamed her "T Hayes." I'm not sure if she reminded us of someone or not. After learning her name, she became a more real person to all of us, and not just a "bag lady!"

At the front desk, I was able to see how other friars relate to their clientele. I got to use my Spanish on occasion. I was at the heart of the action at St. Francis! The lobby, in the same room as the desk, is an experience in itself!

HELPING THOSE IN NEED

How does one help people who do not want to be helped? How does one motivate where there has never been motivation? How does one give someone else self-respect? I honestly came to the conclusion that some street people have chosen this as their way of life, and they prefer it to a life of responsibility and commitment. I do think, however, that each case is different and should be dealt with individually. At times, if one is refused a handout, s/he makes a scene, yelling and cursing all the way down the street. So, it is very difficult to know what is best to do.

Morning Breadline

Any friar coming home after 11:00 P.M. on a summer evening would be certain to meet one of the men who slept on our steps in order to get an early (5:30 A.M.) start on the breadline the next day. Every morning, either two bologna or cheese sandwiches and a cup of coffee were offered to the 350 to 400 men and six to ten women who came to receive it.

In the beginning, this was a romantic apostolate for me. The friars gave out the sandwiches and tried to keep the line orderly. Among these people, Machiavelli's rule of "might makes right" held full sway and switchblades were had by all. No one ever behaved like that toward one of the friars unless the man was a stranger to the breadline. The regulars had great respect for the hands that fed them—and love, too!

I will never forget the first day I gave out the food. I was filled with fear and anticipation as to what the men would be like. They really did not look as sloppy or as tough as I had suspected. They were real people, but poor, and my fears were quickly relieved.

I watched their eyes as they looked at the sandwiches in expectation, how they shone when they had the food in their hands. They said, "Thank you, Father!" I was humbled and said, "Don't thank me. Thank God and the people who paid for them. I'm only passing on what's been given to us, as the minister of these goods."

For some comic relief, after I got to know the men, I sometimes said such things as: "one cheeseburger here," "steak sandwich coming up," "hot roast beef on rye." They got a kick out of it! It was good to see them smile, and it was humanizing to laugh with them. I felt a genuine rapport with the men from the start, and I think they knew I was on their side. Soon afterwards, they began asking me for clothes. We had a steady supply of donated clothing; so I tried to help them out and accommodate them.

I got to know many of the men personally, by standing around after coffee, just being friendly, shooting the breeze with them, treating them like human beings, with respect and reverence. I know they detected the real interest and concern that I had for them, which made me feel good, too!

Hi, Brother!

I could not walk anywhere in the city without coming across one of the men. No matter how I was dressed, in habit or not, they knew me, too, and said "hello." It was truly a good feeling knowing these men considered me their friend!

Their lifestyles bothered me and challenged me. How could anyone live that way? I learned much when I asked them some of my troubling questions, although some men were experts at being vague. I never really knew whether they were telling me the truth. It didn't seem likely that all these men were forced to live this way; some of them must choose it. Some must be running from something.

This work alone could take up one's whole time in the apostolate at St. Francis. Some friars do work with these less fortunate people full time. And I had often considered working with these poor and alcoholic people for my future ministry. My experience with them, although limited, was a real taste of this work.

Other than my relationship with Mr. T., whom I met working on the desk, I will mention two other men.

Kim G. was a "regular" at the breadline, as well as at the wall at Madison Square Garden. The world seemed to take advantage of Kim. The fifty-year-old man came to trust me, and asked me if I would write him a letter of reference to Welfare stating that he had no permanent residence, that he had been sleeping on our steps every night for the past two months. I wrote the letter for him, hoping he would get some benefits from it.

Glen was a young man in his twenties and a friend of Kim. He seemed intelligent, fairly decent, and well groomed. I could never figure out or find out why he lived this way. For some reason, he wanted to get out of the "normal" stream of life for a while.

With Glen, Kim, and many of the other men, I often had interesting conversations about the world, life, the Church, and God.

Senior Citizens

Our duty here entailed setting the tables and chairs, as well as putting together the small food packets we gave to the people. The other young friars and myself devoted every Thursday afternoon from 1:00 P.M. to 4:30 P.M. to these hundred elderly people.

The usual routine consisted of walking around speaking with them, being friendly, smiling, kissing them, or shaking their hands. Some of them were old, tough Irish women whom it took a while to get to know. Many of these people lived in constant fear on the streets of New York, frightened even to stay alone in their homes. These afternoons gave them chances to feel a sense of community or togetherness with other people of the same age. It was great to see them making friends with each other.

Activities on these days included showing movies, singing, or playing Bingo. Once I did my Louis Armstrong imitation for them. They loved it! I felt that it was good to be a fool for them, that they might laugh and have a good time. It was well worth it seeing those old, wrinkled faces smiling.

I regularly listened to their stories and suffered their hardships with them, but I believe I really emptied myself when they held their fair. I conducted the "Bean Bag" game. I tried my best to shout like a carnival barker, to make it more real and fun for them; again, I hoped to bring some joy to them, at a little expense to myself. Often, I knew that the women came to my game because they liked me. They enjoyed acting maternal, treating the young friars like their grandsons. Although it is difficult for me to be the receiver, I allowed them to do this. It gave them a chance to feel their ability to have concern, love, and care for another.

Another outstanding event was the day we went on an outing to a winery in upstate New York. I really did not feel like it, but because they requested it, I led them in singing on the bus. I don't have a good voice, but I do have a big mouth! And I remembered many of their old songs.

The day itself entailed helping them walk and keeping them together. This was burdensome as well as exhausting.

Having done lots of work in nursing homes during my years in the minor seminary, I really did not look forward to our meetings once a week, but I did give myself to them as much as I could. It was pitiful to see the psychological worlds in which some of these people live. Many of them are mentally in another world. To treat them with the love of God was indeed the challenge for me.

Often, some of our apostolates overlapped. For instance, many of our senior citizens were regulars in the Church. Some of them lived in the Aberdeen Hotel which I also visited once a week.

Through attempting to serve these people, I became more aware of the problems of old folks facing suffering and death. I came into contact with the piety and moral conscience formation of an age gone by. I learned some of the fear and loneliness, as well as isolation and alienation that come with growing old in a city like New York. I could also plainly see how people at this age turn to God and religion more out of need than out of free choice. Often I felt in their piety that they were saying: "Lord, to whom else can we go?" (*John* 6).

Aberdeen Welfare Hotel

I walked two blocks away to the Aberdeen at 9:00 A.M. every Thursday morning with Fr. John McVean. My purpose there again was to listen, and to be of whatever help I could to these people. Some were entirely dependent on welfare; others were out-patients from the psychiatric department at Bellevue Hospital. I saw my role as one of witness to the love and concern of God and the Church for these people.

This involved listening to Valeri talk—and keep talking—out loud to me about herself. It required playing cards with seventeen-year-old Harold, who was a manic depressive. It meant trying to get twenty-year-old Cheryl to talk at all to somebody. It meant watching gay Eduardo dance around to rock and roll music. It was trying to patch up a quarrel between Cleopatra and twenty-six-year-old alcoholic, homosexual Lester. Cleopatra named herself because that's who she wanted to be! Basically, I saw myself as trying to support and reinforce positive growth and healthy concerns in these people where I saw them.

There were two people with whom I had two specific religious discussions. These discussions were good, not only because they made the people conscious of the Lord briefly, but also because the discussions seemed to get the whole room of people involved, which I felt was even therapeutic in some ways.

One discussion was with nineteen-year-old Peter, who was a black fundamentalist. He continued to challenge me on the Roman Catholic devotion to the saints, our Blessed Mother, our use of statues, and material things which he considered to be idol worship. I felt this was good, for it made people think, myself included. The only unfortunate part of the discussion, as in all religion discussions, was that people got too excited. I became a referee after a while. Peter was persistent in his views, but often obnoxious, almost as if he never listened to my responses or anyone else's. Peter was a part of my concern over the devotions to the saints, etc., which existed at St. Francis and which I discussed earlier.

Another specific discussion that I felt was extremely worthwhile for me and for all present because of the vitality of the topic happened on the Jewish feast of Yom Kippur. I later used this discussion as a basis for a homily. Mr. R. lamented not being with his people and shared with us his fear of death. It was beautiful to see how the others tried to make him feel not alone but accepted. It was especially inspirational to see how some of the people tried to convince Mr. R. that Jesus Christ died for our sins, rose from the dead, and conquered death. The people were truly good to him, not preachy, but compassionate.

There were some people at the Aberdeen Hotel with whom I developed personal relationships. One was a fifty-year-old Italian woman, Nancy, who was separated from her husband and who drank a bit too much. Nancy invited me to her room. She wanted me to talk to her two children on the telephone and tell them she was all right and that she presently was not drinking. Nancy tried to come to Mass when I preached. She also introduced me to some of her poorer friends, to whom I gave clothes.

Marsha was twenty-three and intelligent. I'm not sure what her problem was. But once, when she was very upset, she came to see me at St. Francis. I helped her put matters in perspective and she was relieved.

Martha belonged to our senior citizen's club and every Thursday she went out to buy donuts for the rest of the people at the Aberdeen. She liked to have me keep her company, so I went with her.

Lucille was middle-aged, black, but better off financially and mentally than many others. She cooked a southern dish for Fr. John and me once (candied yams and ham hocks) and brought it to us at St. Francis. I really made a big fuss over it and thanked her.

Scott was about nineteen and was very withdrawn. He looked so scared and lost, that I felt really sorry for him and wanted to help. He was so young. However, he went back to Bellevue before I got the chance to make any contact.

Old Henry was sixty-three and black. He just smoked cigars, drank, and rode up and down the elevator. At times he came to our breadline in the mornings. I just tried to be friendly to Henry. Though I did not know how to help him, I really liked him.

One very special occasion took place during my last week in New York. Nancy and I spoke about going to see the movie *Jesus Christ Superstar*. Then we decided, why not have all of us go? We got funded by the State and went. I took this as an opportunity to do something spiritual for those who could understand and appreciate it.

And so, before going to the movie, I asked them all to meet in the recreation room. I talked a little bit about Jesus, and how this movie was a modern interpretation of his life. I tried to make sure that they did not think it would be sacrilegious. I asked them to see it as something spiritual. Then I said a little prayer before we all walked five blocks together down 34th Street to the theater.

After the movie, and after many of them told me how much they liked it and how I looked like Jesus did in the movie, we all walked down the street arm-in-arm singing. We all felt united. It was truly one of the most beautiful experiences of community in my life. We brought each person there into the song, by naming him or her. It was indeed a special night, another miracle on 34th Street!

I realized my limitation as a helper with these people, but also that I could, in my own small way, as a human being and as a minister, somehow mediate the saving, loving, caring presence of the Lord to them by doing some of the things I have mentioned. I also glimpsed in them a depth of mental deficiency, as well as emotional problems that I had never seen before. I also realized, however, the limitations of science and the other helping professions in healing these people.

Areas of Resistance

I evaluated myself according to Kenosis and my effectiveness in counseling. My personal measuring sticks were: being available, interpreting needs, helping others to respond to their needs.

Availability: Being available consisted of spending time waiting for people to come to me, overcoming tiredness and fatigue, keeping my own spirit alive on a particular day. I liken the notion of availability to Nouwen's notion of hospitality as presented in his book, *The Wounded Healer*. He says

> Hospitality is the ability to pay attention to the guest. This is very difficult, since we are preoccupied with our own needs, worries and tensions, which prevent us from taking distance from ourselves in order to pay attention to others.[4]

He goes on to say that

> the minister who comes to terms with his own loneliness (implying other problems and wounds here) and is at home in his own house (self) is a host who offers hospitality to his guests. He gives them a friendly space where they may feel free to come and go, to be close and distant, to rest and to play, to talk and to be silent.[5]

Maybe availability and hospitality can be summed up in the word "readiness." When a person came for help, was I ready for him/her? To what extent was I in touch with myself? Were all of my pastoral skills ready and at my disposal to serve? Was my theology and my pastoral sense integrated and ready to be implemented?

These were some of the ambiguities and perplexities I experienced in preparing myself for counseling. I cannot remember a day that I was totally unprepared. Days varied, as all human days do, but some days I was more available and some days I was less ready and less hospitable because of some preoccupation. I would say, however, that generally I was ready and anxious to be present, and to welcome others into redemptive space with me. I have already mentioned the two weeks in which I had no counseling duty because no one came. This influenced my attitude a bit. The third week I was overly anxious and a trifle preoccupied about whether my availability would be wasted that day. I tried to be calm and I think I was. Some people came that day, but I don't think I communicated any of this frustration to them. I was hospitable.

The Other's Need: Interpreting the need of the person is the second factor to be evaluated. I know I am more prepared for spiritual counseling and enjoy it more. So I had to be careful not to impose my ability to serve, to inflict spiritual problems on to what was needed by the person. If the person needed information about Church teaching, I should not convert the session into a therapeutic relationship. If the person needed to pray with someone, I should not resist because of my own embarrassment at sharing personal prayer. Half the chore of a good counselor is interpreting where the need is. It is not always what the person says it is either. Here is where training and a keen ear become important, as I learned from my sessions with Fr. Blaise. I must not listen so much to content, but to the feeling behind what the person is saying.

This might imply getting persons to deeper points in their lives than they had initially bargained for. This is part of the risk the counselor takes. S/he must interpret. S/he must take calculated risks according to that interpretation. This is why the counselor must not be self-imposing, if possible. S/he must be purified of his/her own desire for ego success. Kenosis is indeed a prerequisite for counseling. The counselor must be free of self in order to interpret the client's need and take steps to remedy those needs, wherever the direction of risk might personally take the counselor.

Through feedback from Fr. Blaise, I know that I am fairly sensitive in listening. He told me I am empathetic. However, he also told me that I often seem too directive. For instance, I might ask a person to pray at the end of a session, but Fr. Blaise wondered if that was for the person's good, or for my own need to feel spiritual, that I was helping in a religious way. He told me I have many talents in the area of counseling, but that I must sharpen myself as a healing instrument. More experience and learning would help.

Their Responsibility: Helping others respond to their needs was indeed a chore for me. Often I took too much of the burden rather than leaving it for the person to carry with my help. I often took the other's problems too seriously. I sometimes became depressed or overly preoccupied with a particular case so that it influenced the other areas of my life. I think I am growing and maturing as a counselor here.

I always try to help the person realize his/her own power to be healed, if this is realistic. I do not want people to be dependent, even though at times this is a start to becoming more independent, i.e., by depending and believing in me and, therefore, in someone.

When people needed me to listen, I listened. When they needed advice, I gave it. When they needed someone more experienced or competent than myself, I obtained these people for them or told them where they might get help. In general, I think I responded well to their needs, and generally tried to make these people feel responsibility for their own selves and their own healing. Often, this is very difficult to do, for they are seeking security and often we "helpers" are seeking to be needed. My experience of Kenosis is indeed one of self-purification in counseling.

I learned a great deal that summer through counseling. Fr. Blaise told me I had great potential. I am interested in developing that potential, as a counselor, as a future confessor, as a pastor in general.

Information desk: The main thrust on the desk was a real ministry of "personal witness" and welcome.

Often when it got busy, and long lines began to form, I found myself becoming more and more businesslike. This was difficult to overcome. The people got anxious at these times and tended to make me anxious also.

Another part of this duty on the desk was to try and educate the people in very limited ways about religious things such as the Mass through Mass cards. The challenge was to try to convert their sometimes superstitious attitudes toward the Mass to a more faithful notion of what the Eucharist is really all about. This was my attitude more than my practice because in truth we had very little time to spend or chat with each person. A smile or some kindness was about all there was time for on days like that.

As can be seen from my previous description of the experiences on the desk, I handled it fairly well. There were times when I was just too exhausted to put out much love or kindness. There were times, however, when I overcame this fatigue and gave all that I could at that time.

Breadline: Resisting Kenosis here would mean not respecting the men on the breadline, treating them with pity, like the "poor" that we felt sorry for and looked down on. This is why I enjoyed joking with the men and speaking with them. I know they detected that I was treating them as equals with dignity.

When some of the men attempted to flatter me, saying how holy we friars are, or other things like this, they appreciated my telling them to stop putting us above them. They also knew I could see through what they were saying and didn't enjoy that type of talk, as they had expected I might.

Senior Citizens: The biggest criticism of myself in this area was that after I got to know many of the old folks, I usually spent time with the people I liked. The minister must go not only where he likes, but where he is needed.

Often I tried to get by with the least amount of output as possible. These people expected very little and were content with the slightest effort. Sometimes this was all I gave. They also could see right through someone if he was too sweet with them. They wanted a real, live person, not a phony. At times, as a defense, I know I came on as too nice.

One difficulty I had was knowing how to challenge these old people. Maybe the question was whether I should challenge them or not. Some of them were obviously prejudiced in the way they spoke about the "colored." They had lived seventy years with these attitudes, often in fear in this big city. How does one address this problem? With sympathy for their plight, not pointing out to them their prejudice? Or should it be brought up? They might agree verbally, but their gut feelings would change very little. Kenosis here demanded discernment. What good would come from a discussion about race? Who am I, a twenty-five-year-old

Christian, to tell them about how to be Christian when they've been Christians, according to their definition, for seventy years? Kenosis often implies presuming good faith, whether that faith is based on experience or ignorance, and deciding from there what to say or do. I feel that if I do not think challenging will help a person grow, then it is not worth it.

Aberdeen Hotel: In general, I was often depressed at the thought of going to the Aberdeen, knowing I would be absolutely drained in the short span of three hours spent there, listening to these people and attempting to be present to them. What good was I doing anyway? I often had to overcome many feelings in order to walk those two short blocks to the hotel with Fr. John. Knowing that I was supporting him in his work and that perhaps I might do something worthwhile for someone that morning motivated me to go. I often questioned if my suffering there was redemptive? Was anyone really benefiting from my presence? What I had to realize was that my criteria for feeling useful were not always their criteria for being helped or feeling better. Even though I felt discouraged by the personal cost and little response, often my very presence there did help someone. Fr. John was a great help in reflecting on this experience with me and encouraging me.

At the Aberdeen, I was placed in the priest role. The patients did not treat me as a person, but as someone unreal. They would "yes Father" me to death. As a result, I often did not know what they were really feeling or thinking. Perhaps this is an occupational hazard.

It was difficult maintaining a discussion with them. I did not understand enough about each of their cases to know whether to take them seriously or not. On our walk back to St. Francis, Fr. John and I usually discussed the morning spent at the Aberdeen.

On the evening we went to see *Superstar*, I felt a bit paternalistic being with these people and walking with them to the movie. I wanted to see them as my brothers and sisters and treat them equally, but somehow I felt a sense of distance from them. I was self-emptying, but I guess one could say that it was here where I might have "clung to my divinity" (normality?). I was embarrassed to be with one of these patients, a Jewish man named Donald. He was one who constantly demanded my attention, while he continuously asked religious questions. The problem was that he was persistent and obnoxious, and he never really listened to my answers. I guess one could say I truly felt my limitation for self-emptying here. He was very hard to take. I found it difficult to be patient with him. The other residents noticed this and sympathized with me either through their words or looks.

In general, I felt good about the Aberdeen experience and that I never allowed myself to stop going there on Thursday mornings. Persevering in this service I felt a bit of the pain in never allowing "love to give up" (1 *Cor.* 13).

Ramifications for Ministry

Theologically, I learned that the minister deals with people whose faith is on many different levels. Some people I served had no explicit faith. Some had very explicit, but perhaps stilted faith. I learned that I have to meet people at their faith level, encourage whatever I find of faith there, and attempt to help them grow in it.

I learned that even though I am an explicit minister of Jesus Christ, and of the Catholic Church, that I will meet and serve people who use different words for perhaps the same realities or values for which I stand. There are many "anonymous Christians" in the world who may be even more successful in helping God's Kingdom break in than I am. I must relate to these positive movements of love and truth in people, and share the vision that we have in common so we can continue to build God's dream together!

I also learned a certain caution: one must be very careful about dealing with people who are innocently living in good faith, but who might be doing something wrong or might have misconceptions about faith. I think I have come to realize that it is only worthwhile causing a disturbance in someone's faith life if one is reasonably sure that this person is capable of growth. Otherwise, I do not think it is wise. I really have no right disturbing someone living in good faith, unless I or someone else will be around afterwards to help the pieces fit back together again in a new way.

This informal ministry took me into areas (old age, mental health, poverty) where God could easily be slapped on to problems as the solution. I found that we cannot just use God as a Band-Aid! I would have felt I was being unjust to these people if I talked about

God and religion to them all the time, and yet did not help them to deal more effectively with their lives.

Dressed either in Roman collar or Franciscan habit, I, in a very real sense, was religion to them. I might have been their only experience of the Good News, in my concern, care, in my "being with" them, in my "pitching my tent" among them. This was God's presence among them. I know it! Did I have to label it with theological terms for their sake or mine? No, I do not think so. But I should not avoid that either, if called for. To live and express religion genuinely is no easy task. There exist many variables which must be taken into account. The other person's state of maturity, capacity for growth, openness, and need must all be considered seriously in ministry.

Ministry had told me that there are many grass roots which have to be planted and nourished for the reality of the Kingdom to blossom. The sign of the Kingdom's presence is a multi-faceted one, involving both the physical and spiritual:

> Go and report to John what you have seen and heard. The blind recover their sight, cripples walk, lepers are cured, the deaf hear, dead men are raised to life, and the poor have the good news preached to them (*Luke* 7: 22).

It seems that we must minister to both body and soul if we are to follow the example of the Master. Sometimes, however, it becomes frustrating when it seems that some people have such huge physical problems that one can never address their spiritual ones.

Obviously, however, I do not believe that ministers must heal bodies first before dealing with souls. I think that both can be done simultaneously. However, it is often my frustration to find that I very rarely get beyond pre-evangelization in the informal ministry to more direct or explicit sharing of the Gospel message. I agree that this in itself is valid ministry. My only regret is not being able to directly preach, explicitly proclaim the Good News in sophisticated language. Maybe this is good, for it forces me to translate that Good Word into flesh, making it comprehensible for the poorest and littlest ones.

I felt the need for a more conscious direction, coordinating the efforts of all the friars involved in these informal ministries at St. Francis. I feel that theological goals ought to be set up and more consciously striven toward together, as a group of men working for the Kingdom. I think that more conscious sharing of goals and vision would add much impetus to the great work already being done there.

I learned that there is a constant need to be informed about referral agencies. The minister must know to whom he can send people.

I also learned, however, that there is much I can do as a minister, which I did not have the confidence to do before. I learned that often people cannot afford to be referred, and that we may be their only hope for any growth. Ministers must take themselves and their counseling roles seriously.

Awareness of my role as a minister and friar and how to be comfortable in it were other professional insights I gained. Adjustments must often be made in one's projection of one's role image. These should be made according to an authentic understanding of one's professional identity, plus what one interprets as the people's need. As in faith and other areas of ministry, the same holds for one's professional identity—there is a give-and-take between the self of the minister and the others to whom he ministers.

I definitely discovered in informal ministry the depth of my experience. I suffered in this area the most, I wondered the most, I was challenged the most, and I grew the most!

I came to the realization that I cannot love from some ivory tower, that I must not merely use words but action. We must "love in deed and in truth and not merely talk about it" (1 *John* 3: 18). As he had laid down his life for us, we too ought to "lay down our lives for our brothers" (1 *John* 3: 16).

Even if results are not apparent or immediate, we must have hope of eschatological or future completion:

> Let us not grow weary of doing good; if we do not relax our efforts, in due time we shall reap our harvest. While we have the opportunity, let us do good to all . . . but especially those of the household of the faith (*Gal.* 6: 9).

I have to admit that it is within the context of informal ministry that I learned the meaning of the words I uttered the day I was first vested in the garb of St. Francis, the words that enable me to express the unity with the Lord Jesus and the world which I have come to experience in ministry through the prism of Kenosis:

May I never boast of anything but the cross of our Lord Jesus Christ! Through it, the world has been crucified to me and I to the world (*Gal.* 6: 14).

MY OWN SPECIAL MINISTRY

This was a personal ministry adopted as the summer went on. It was a ministry I engaged in at times between my ordinary assigned duties at St. Francis, or on my own time off. I considered it to be an apostolate of witness. And I did it as a personal experiment.

I believe that a city like New York is badly in need of some Christian witness. I find it to be a city caught up in itself, perhaps as the earthly paradise, a place where skin flicks are advertised on every street, a place where people rush, shove, kick each other to get where they are going. It's a place where money is the god adored, where people treat each other like things, using each other to their own advantage. It seems to be a place where false gods and false religions are not only publicly solicited, but publicly accepted, advertised, and encouraged.

In a city like this, I felt the need and desire to give some kind of physical, external, public witness to transcendence, to the spiritual, to the heavenly Jerusalem, to a God who is love, who values persons over things, who gives peace and rest to the weary and the broken.

Although there has been much talk since Vatican II about getting the clergy out of the rectory and into the lives of the people, I have found that this is not really being done in New York City. I felt that my special ministry was one "of the marketplace," one where the minister does not wait for people to come to the Church, but rather the Church goes to the people—the Church and the Lord through my ministry.

I am often impressed by the commitment and external desire of other groups who want to share publicly with the world what they believe. In New York City the Hare Krishna, whom I found both on Broadway and on 34th Street, is one such group. Another group with a street outreach program was the Church of Scientology. These people were in the subways, on the streets; they seemed to be everywhere! Many other groups came and went.

However, I did not like either the obnoxious ways these people seemed to proselytize, their narrow-mindedness, nor their pressure tactics in inducing others to buy their product: their religion. They seemed more inclined towards brainwashing than towards respecting human dignity and freedom. I also did not enjoy the way many Christians and fallen-away Catholics were joining these groups.

Street Walking

What I did was take walks in the Franciscan habit, either by myself or with other friars. I walked around the block, near Macy's, or down to the Port Authority on 8th Avenue and 42nd Street, or up to a prayer meeting on 67th Street and Lexington Avenue. Or, I merely stood outside the church and friary in between Masses, or in the afternoons when people were on their way home after work. I went to Madison Square Garden on the evenings of rock concerts and mingled with the teenagers while they were waiting for the doors to open. I tried to smile, to seem peaceful and friendly to people. I stopped and talked with anyone whom I interpreted as showing some kind of interest or curiosity. I preferred that they take the initiative; otherwise I would have felt that I was forcing myself on people.

The practical dimensions of this Kenosis are perhaps the most difficult of all of the others already mentioned. This Kenosis demands that one not only be ready and hospitable to people, but almost that one advertise this availability. I remember a prayer card once which read: ''Availability is the sign of a soul completely free.'' This particular work required being available and being free.

The dimensions of this type of ministry demand a certain quality and depth in the person regarding his growth in the other forms of Kenosis mentioned in this book. This Kenosis requires proficiency and quality in the others. This was different from a ministry in the Church. In this special ministry, I experienced the reactions of people quite overtly—what they felt towards God and the Church—because I was their representative to the world.

Having My Act Together

This Kenosis demanded that I be reconciled in myself, be relatively at peace with myself in every way, and with the Lord. Then I had to be willing to try and make that reconciliation available to whoever might feel the Lord calling. This risk meant being ready to be stared at, laughed at, ridiculed, scorned, treated like a fool! Fundamentally, this Kenosis challenged me to put myself "on the line," to go to the capital of the world, to the marketplace as the representative of Jesus Christ, the Roman Catholic Church, and the Franciscan Order! And to be ready for the consequences! This Kenosis obviously required a commitment to the Lord, to the Church, and to the Order of Friars Minor. This Kenosis involved a true desire to share with others the good things the Lord has given me, the minister. It demanded a real love for people as my sisters and brothers if it was to be authentic, if it was to work at all.

And so in summary, let me say that this special ministry required some proficiency in the other forms of Kenosis, the desire to risk sharing that proficiency, a true sense of commitment to what the minister was representing, a true readiness to give whatever someone needed, and a true love for others in order to be willing to take such a risk.

Meeting Them Where They Were

My approach with people was very low key. My attitude was to meet them where they were. I seldom made a direct initiative. I believe in the quiet, peaceful, personal approach to people and to groups. I did not want to push myself on anyone. I wanted to be a sign of the Lord's presence, available to them, but not forced on them. I wanted to give people someone to respond to. I did not hand out leaflets, or propaganda, but was just there by myself, hopefully as a living Gospel and as a potential Word made flesh. I was happy to see this approach and attitude of ministry which I had confirmed in a document of the General Chapter of the Order of Friars Minor which says:

> As witnesses to the Gospel, it is not our lot, in our contacts with people, to indulge in disputes or to practice proselytism,

even of a religious nature; we wish simply to be peace-
makers, without pretention, courteous, joyful, submissive to
everyone, practicing non-resistance if necessary, remaining
convinced that we are the Servants of the Word that is far
greater than we. By a love both lucid and gentle, we must
bear witness to the pricelessness of each person.[6]

That was why it was so necessary for me to summon all my
sensitivities together. First of all, I wanted to be sensitive to how
people were responding to me. Secondly, after the initial contact, I
tried to be as present as possible in whatever way I felt that the
person needed me.

I will not go into cases in detail, but I will discuss people based
on the number of times I saw them and the effect I think our meeting had. I think that it is necessary to mention some of these situations, so as to give an idea of this ministry. The three categories
I will use are: many times, more than once, and only one time.

Many Times: I would categorize the people I saw many times after
the initial contact as: permanently influenced, street people,
passersby.

Permanently influenced: Jim and I met on our front steps. He
told me he was seeking God and the Church again, that he had
fallen away. He was twenty-three years old. Jim and I had an
ongoing relationship. We went to prayer meetings together, discussed God and Scripture.

Anthony and I met in our bookstore where we struck up a
conversation. He told me he had tried yoga and many other ways
to help him grow and find himself. Now he had been baptized in
the Holy Spirit and was attempting to be a real Christian again. It
was through him that I began to go to the charismatic prayer
meetings.

Bill told me one day outside our church on 32nd Street that he
had seen me four or five times walking around the block and that
he had always wanted to talk to me. He could not believe, because
of my appearance, that I was allowed to be a friar. A simple conversation such as that led Bill, twenty-four years old, to reveal his
whole life to me. He went to the minor seminary for two years with
another religious order. He began to use drugs in high school, was
responsible for and felt guilty about four young people who died
of overdoses. Now he was no longer a junkie, but was presently

supporting his townhouse on the upper East Side through what he called "his girls." Bill was a pimp. I saw him three or four times after this and discussed his present life, his spiritual life, and his future.

I met Mike on our front steps after seeing *Superstar*. It turned out that this nineteen-year-old had run away from a drug rehabilitation center in Newark, and wanted to try to make it on his own in New York City. He had been sleeping in alleyways for three nights. I gave Mike a clean set of clothes, a shower, and then we walked over to McDonald's for something to eat. I put him up in my room that night. I saw Mike each day of that week. He worked for Manpower (a part-time job agency). After getting to know him, seeing his potential, and realizing that this was my last week in New York, I knew I had to bring up the alternatives to Mike. Either he was going to make it on his own (which I told him I doubted, for New York is a rough place to be without money or friends), or he could go back to the drug center, or he could go back to drugs. I had been building up his confidence. It was very difficult for me to face him with these possible realities.

Street People: As I have already mentioned, whenever I went out I met some of these people on the street, in a park, or at Madison Square Garden.

Maureen used to stand down on the corner of 31st Street, where St. Francis was. She was filthy, always talking or cursing, but never making sense. I was the first one to learn her name. We eventually spoke a little more sensibly. I felt that she needed someone to care. I tried.

Elizabeth stood near our doorway on 32nd Street. She used to beg there. I got to know her and challenged her to work for she was still young and healthy.

Whenever I could, I tried to be on our friary steps when work let out, around 4:30–5:30 every afternoon. It surprised me how many regular faces, "hellos," and smiles people began to give back.

One young man, who worked across the street, presented me with a marriage problem once because he saw me as someone friendly.

People often showed concern for me, especially when I was sunburned. People said things such as, "Father, you better put some lotion on that." "Out in the sun, eh Father?" These comments told me it was worthwhile. Something was happening!

More than once: Joseph was a young Mormon who seemed to need a friend. I met him on our front steps. I could never figure out why he kept coming back to see me. We often talked religion, for he used to be a Catholic.

Flavia was a fifteen-year-old who came up to me on the steps one day, crying. I thought someone had died in her family. She was just so happy to see a young person like me involved with religion. She seemed to feel happy over our two or three talks.

Alex was an out-patient from Creedmoor Mental Hospital whom I also met on our front steps. He now worked for the nearby New York Post Office. We often talked about religion, problems with his sexuality, and his loneliness.

I met Marie one day at the back entrance to the church. She began telling me about her daughter who has mental problems. It turned out that I knew her daughter from the Aberdeen Hotel. We discussed her daughter's life and her development the other two times we met.

One time: I met Mark at the corner of 7th Avenue and 32nd Street. He asked me for directions. We got into a discussion about how he just had a very deep religious experience induced by LSD the night before. We walked back to the church, had some coffee, and talked for two hours. It seemed like a genuine religious experience to me. This led to our speaking about his spiritual life, etc.

Brian, like many others I met, began our discussion antagonistically. The typical bombshells seem to be the infallibility of the Pope, the wealth of the Church, the Blessed Mother, and the saints. This young man was a Jesus freak of sorts. I tried to focus on areas where we were united rather than divided. Brian used to be Catholic. I imagine, to him as to the other young ex-Catholics, I represented the possibility of Catholicism.

Dominic and Anthony were both sitting near Madison Square Garden when we began to talk. They complained about how irrelevant the Church was to them, especially the Mass at their home parish which was terrible and boring. Their religion courses at St. John's University they found to be of limited worth. I acknowledged their problems, but also challenged their personal faith and effort.

Three lawyers waiting to take their law boards were sitting outside the Hilton on 8th Avenue during a coffee break. They asked me if I was some kind of monk. With that introduction one can go in many directions. I began to explain to them what my life meant—the Gospel, celibacy, the Church, the knots on my cord, etc. We spoke much about sexuality. Celibacy stumped them! So, what's new?

Often I was just a sounding board for the person. Jerry, a Pentecostal, shared his enthusiasm about the Lord. Mike, a soldier, told me about war and his time in Vietnam.

At times it seemed like I was wasting my time. A young black, T.J., who was taught by Capuchins Friars and so recognized the habit, thought he was my greatest friend and protector against any trouble near the Garden. I thought maybe our relationship might help him, but when I saw him again he did not even remember me. Maybe I was just another "high" in one of his drug trips.

Other times I met crazy or neurotic people who had no ability to carry on a conversation, or to make any response at all. Some of them just kept asking questions. I did not know what to do with these people.

Areas of Resistance

I found different attitudes in myself, which I gave into, and which were adverse to this ministry. At times, even though I was convinced of the worth of this apostolate, I succumbed to the real or imaginary criticism or disapproval of other friars. I had a sense that my doing this made some other friars uncomfortable. Maybe they were embarrassed to have me represent the Order and the Church in such a public way.

Sometimes, even though I knew something good was happening in this apostolate, I allowed myself to be inhibited by others.

Other times, I just was not in the mood to overcome my fears, and so I did not go out to the steps or people. Some friars think that it was easy for me to do this ministry. Perhaps this ministry was more suited to only my personality. However, there was not one time when I went out that it did not take courage, and lots of it—all I had!

In dealing with the people, occasionally I felt myself labeling them immediately, perhaps because of their outward appearances. I did not feel that this was kenotic. Other times, I greeted someone too curtly or gruffly.

The nature of this ministry demanded I remain sensitive and aware of the atmosphere that I was in with a person at every moment. Sometimes, however, I was guilty of what I would call "roaming eyes." While I was supposedly present and talking to someone, I might be looking all around, not listening at all to that person, which was the whole purpose of this ministry and Kenosis —to be there, present, for the other.

Potential dangers in this ministry were being defensive or narrow-minded with people, selling my product obnoxiously, or a possible ego trip by being the center of attention. These dangers were not that real to me, although I can imagine their possibilities in my own life.

I also had to contend with the constant tension of avoiding sensationalism or huge crowds. And, I had to resist the desire to save everybody, to be content with simply reaching only one person every time I went out.

Ramifications for Ministry

Since the nature of this ministry was really experimental, I found two practical results which would have, in my opinion, ramifications for ministry.

In looking over the journal in which I recorded every person I spoke to or dealt with, I discovered that I met as many people in this special ministry as I did in any one of the other particular ministries, such as counseling, preaching, the Aberdeen Hotel, etc. I not only met with these people, but think that I had more significant relationships with them which had definite bearing on their lives. This tells me that there is a good possibility of "the marketplace" being a thriving ministry.

This has particular significance for me as a Friar Minor and a mendicant. I found that what I was doing was in tune with the spirit of both the Church and our Order, as is noted in the articles of our provincial chapter of 1969, *Rebuild My House*, concerning new apostolates:

Pope Paul VI has summoned the Church with an ever-increasing urgency for more positive pastoral involvement, which will necessitate new and imaginative forms of ministry. Openness of structure, imaginative pastoral response, mobility in ministry, dedication to the estranged and to the poor—all these are the authentic traditions of the Franciscan Order.[7]

I found this apostolate to be pastoral, free of structure, mobile, and spontaneous—very Franciscan. I found it to be resonant with the call of Vatican II in *Perfectae Caritatis* to go back to the spirit of our founder. This ministry told me that it is possible today to go back not only in word, but in action, to the simple way of ministry of St. Francis, who once told Brother Leo to accompany him on a preaching trip through a nearby town. They walked through the whole town silently and Francis called this "preaching by their example."

I was also astounded in reviewing my journal to find that the majority of people who stopped me in the streets to talk were either nonpracticing or fallen-away Catholics. They seemed to be taken aback by a young, bearded friar who believed in Jesus Christ, by someone who was a member of the Catholic Church and still believed in it, and who also had hope for it. People would say such things as: "I never knew they had young friars!" or "Do they really let you look like that?" I found that this "marketplace ministry" or "street ministry" so appealed to fallen-away Catholics that I thought of renaming it as "the ministry that seeks out the lost children of the House of Rome."

My frustration was that once these Catholics, usually young ones, warmed up to me and perhaps became open again to the Church, I did not know what to do with them. Where could I tell them to go for good Liturgy? Where is there a really fine parish or Christian community near to where they lived? My knowledge of the New York metropolitan area and Christian activity was not yet that good. Often these people were turned off by the Church, which to them was equivalent to their parish priests. Yet, we had no real programs I could recommend at St. Francis either. This is an area where definite investigation would have to take place for this ministry to be continued, or for it to be successful in the future.

I found that this ministry was answering the Lord's request to not hide our lamps under bushel baskets, not keep our lights hidden, but "so that they may see the goodness in your acts and give praise to your Heavenly Father" (*Matt.* 5: 15–16).

I found that this ministry was an answer to the call of the Lord to preach the Good News in action to the ends of the earth, to the people who ordinarily are not touched because they do not any longer, or never did, go to church.

I found it to be a direct challenge to me theologically to explain in nonelitist, unsophisticated terminology exactly who I was and what I stood for, usually in response to a question such as: "Hey, what's your bag?"

I see this ministry as a very possible one for me in the future. I feel that it is both a challenge to myself, and a challenge to the Order of Friars Minor, as well as to the whole Church to reach out to the unchurched and the alienated.

Professional Learning

Professionally, this ministry gave me an opportunity to practice sensitivity, to size up a person rather quickly. It gave me practice also in communication skills, both in initially meeting with people, as well as in expressing who I am, for whom and what I stand for.

In reacting to people who did not take me seriously, I also learned to have patience. Many of them, in these early stages of conversation, were trying to see what I was made of, to see if they wanted to go any further or deeper.

This ministry deeply challenged me to clarify my own role with regard to my identity inwardly, and how it is that I ought to express myself outwardly to people. I think I also learned how to assert myself in a conversation and perhaps direct it to what might be a more fruitful area of dynamic discussion.

I felt that the skills of all the other ministries mentioned in this book were summoned to the fore in my marketplace ministry, and these skills of counseling, preaching, listening, suffering, being sensitive, all had to be ready to be implemented. I felt that this ministry was the most challenging to me because it demanded the most of me, personally, spiritually, theologically, and professionally.

If nothing else were accomplished in this ministry, I know at least that I was a witness after the manner of St. Francis who one day walked through the streets of a city with a brother and never said a word. I know I was a witness to the sacred in the secular city of New York which is greatly in need of this witness.

But like Francis, I believe I witnessed to the few people I met that a greater future lay ahead of them than the one proposed to them by other people.

I believe that I witnessed to the goodness and holiness of the world, by being a "professionally sacred person," walking among them, among the sinners, the outcasts, the ugly of the city. I believe that this is a ministry of hope, that people are worth it, and that God's Word "I love you" to us humans is still dying (Kenosis) to be made flesh to every single individual through God's ministers. He is still seeking to dwell among us, if people would only open the doors of their hearts to let him come in, to sit among, and to dine with them (*Rev.* 3: 20). This implies a theology of hope and a theology of the world that is not satisfied to be contained in a book, but must be expressed in the active ministry of a real person in the center of the marketplace.

Conclusion: Only Once Perfectly

I learned so much through this pastoral experience and reflection, this adventure of Kenosis. I am sure that I could write one hundred pages more. There is much that I have already gained from it, and yet I even hope to gain more. Some of my final reflections are the following:

By trying to love, trying to empty myself for others in ministry, I think I learned something of the mystery of Christ. I learned how the Lord had so much that He wanted to give, and yet found so few willing or able to receive. I learned something of the Kenosis experienced in giving that self-gift away, hoping that someone will receive it. I learned my own limitation as a giver in comparison to Jesus, both in my willingness to give and in my capability to give successfully.

This experience has taught me to try to be more open to that fullness which all of us have already received (*John* 1: 16). I learned that as the minister attempts to do what Jesus did, he must set his face toward Jerusalem, as Jesus did (*Luke* 9: 51). The minister must realize that in some ways he is going to his own crucifixion. If they did these things to the Master, they will certainly do them to the servant, for "no servant is greater than his Master" (*John* 15: 20). It taught me to realize myself as a servant, and that after serving and giving all I have, I must say with the rest: "We are useless servants, who have only done no more than our duty" (*Luke* 17: 10).

It has taught me that suffering and Kenosis have eschatological effects and redemptive value. It has taught me my need to rely on his promise in his service that

I consider the sufferings of the present time unworthy to be compared with the glory that is to come (*Romans* 8: 18).

There were times when I wanted to empty myself, and did. There were times when I wanted to, but did not know how to, or was not sure if it was worth the risk. There were times when I wanted to, but did not. There were times when I did not want to, yet did. And there were times when I did not want to, and did not.

But I have felt something of what it means to fall to the ground and die, and possibly to bring forth some fruit (*John* 12: 24). And I have felt something of what it means to find one's life by losing it (*John* 12: 25).

I know that through all of this I not only came to grips with who I am as a human, a Christian, a friar, and a minister, but I came to share this with others, and perhaps furthered the experience of redemption. But most importantly, through the prism of Kenosis, and attempting myself to minister and love, I came to know a bit more intimately and personally that "God who is Love" (1 *John* 4: 8) and him who "emptied himself completely unto death on the cross" (*Phil.* 2: 7).

I have begun to understand the greatness of that one "by whose wounds we were healed" (*Isaiah* 53: 5). And I have been consoled in my humanness that seeks to hold back rather than to give, to withdraw rather than to share, to save rather than empty itself, when I recall that there was only one human who ever could, or ever did, completely give himself to the will of his Holy Father God. There was only one man who gave himself completely to his sisters and brothers until there was nothing left to give. There is only one man who, at the end of a life of total self-gift and total Kenosis, could ever be able to say with full confidence, courage, and conviction those three simple words, knowing that He had emptied till there was nothing left, enabling him to say, in that last redemptive gift of breath: "It is finished" (*John* 19: 30).

Epilogue

One might wonder at the closing of these pages: What has happened to this young friar since the summer of '73? Does he still believe in Kenosis and practice it? Does he still view life through its crystal-clear prism? Where is he now?

He was ordained to the priesthood September 14, 1974, on the feast of the Exaltation of the Cross! He'd love to tell all about where he's been and how he's been since. He could call it "Join the friars and see the world!" For his first eight years after ordination, he was stationed in downtown Boston, at St. Anthony Shrine, Arch Street, a "service church" even busier than St. Francis in New York.

He's been to the Holy Land, Rome, and Assisi, once through an anonymous gift. Keep it up, Lord! And since his first trip, he's brought other pilgrims to Rome and Assisi three times. He was chaplain on the QE 2 three times to the Caribbean—a terrible Kenosis, but someone had to do it! He's been given parish missions —one to the youth of Barbados, another difficult assignment! He substituted once for a friar on vacation in San Juan, Puerto Rico for two weeks. And he had a truly kenotic experience for six weeks at the friars' mission church of Our Lady of the Angels, Molynes Road, Kingston, Jamaica. He spent three summers at the St. Francis soup kitchen in Philadelphia, coordinating the volunteer program.

He could call the past seventeen years of Kenosis "Why He Stays." So many friars he was taught by, or who were peers along the journey, have left the Order and some even the Church. For four years he lived in the parish in which he was born, Holy Cross, Soundview Avenue, Bronx, New York. From that friary he worked as the vocation director or recruiter for the Franciscans on the East Coast. It was his privilege to be there with young men who were discerning whether they should "come and see," walk alongside the friars in the footsteps of the Gospel. That job alone would be enough to make one wonder why he stayed, juggling the young men's dreams and inspirations with the reality and visions of the Order of Friars Minor today!

He could call it "Here's looking at you." After vocation ministry, he was gifted with a year-long sabbatical, when he spent time looking at some of the unresolved conflicts and loose ends of his life through counseling. A year when he spent time living alone as a hermit in prayer, study, and contemplation, going into the caves of his life, much like Francis used to go to his, on the heights of Mt. Subasio. A year when he spent time reading and searching out the most powerful influences on our society today—the media explosion in twentieth-century America—studying at New York University and Berkeley.

Or he could call these past years "Perfect Joy"! Having missed the pastoral dimension of his ministry when working in the vocation office, he sought to become more involved with ordinary people again. He had often said that he never joined the Order to be a parish priest. Yet that's where he's been for the past four years, a member of the pastoral team consisting of three friars and six laypeople, at St. Mary's Church, Pompton Lakes, New Jersey, only forty-five minutes from Broadway and 31st Street! It's a very warm, welcoming, forward-looking parish enabling its community to celebrate the Christian life in the Diocese of Paterson.

Yes, he'd call the past seventeen years of priesthood and twenty-two years of Franciscan life "Perfect Joy"!

As he leaves you, he thanks you for accompanying him on part of his journey. He hopes you have been informed a bit, fascinated maybe, or even stretched as you examined both his life and yours through the microscopic lens of Kenosis. He hopes that you have found some of your story in this part of his!

The final thought he wishes to leave with you is perhaps the very starting point all over again! It's a story from *The Little Flowers of St. Francis.* It's one that makes him cry whenever he reads it. Tears come to his eyes at this very moment as he writes, just thinking about it. The story he has wept over when sharing it with others he has loved in Boston, The Bronx, Philadelphia, and Assisi.

It's the story once again of the mystery of Kenosis, of its cost, its view, its pain, and its vision of how things really are. Not

St. Francis at the birdbath, where most would like to leave him.

I don't quite understand this story yet. Nor am I sure that I even agree with its conclusion. All I know is that it makes me cry. Perhaps Francis is crazy! Perhaps he is the richest poorman, the wisest madman? Not many people would agree with his definition of Perfect Joy, or even begin to comprehend it. Maybe that's the power in it that makes me cry! Or perhaps his simple desire to feel what Jesus felt makes me weep, that he felt it, or that I sometimes feel it?

I hope it brings a tear to your eye as it stretches us once more, our minds and our hearts! I hope it invites you once again to take up your life and live it! I hope it calls you into a dream, a journey, a vision, and a prism we've only just begun to see through.

Welcome to a tear and a smile, as we "plainly and simply" hear the story once again. May the tears welcome you, as they rebaptize your eyes into a clearer vision and a more perfect joy!

PERFECT JOY OF ST. FRANCIS

One winter day St. Francis was coming to St. Mary of the Angels from Perugia with Brother Leo, and the bitter cold made them suffer keenly. St. Francis called to Brother Leo, who was walking a bit ahead of him, and he said: "Brother Leo, even if the Friars Minor in every country give a great example of holiness and integrity and good edification, nevertheless write down and note carefully that perfect joy is not in that."

And when he had walked on a bit, St. Francis called him again, saying: "Brother Leo, even if a Friar Minor gives sight to the blind, heals the paralyzed, drives out devils, gives hearing back to the deaf, makes the lame walk, and restores speech to the dumb, and what is still more, brings back to life a man who has been dead four days, write that perfect joy is not in that."

And going on a bit, St. Francis cried out again in a strong voice: "Brother Leo, if a Friar Minor knew all languages and all sciences and Scripture, if he also knew how to prophesy and to reveal not only the future but also the secrets of the consciences and minds of others, write down and note carefully that perfect joy is not in that."

And as they walked on, after a while St. Francis called again forcefully: "Brother Leo, little lamb of God, even if a Friar Minor could speak with the voice of an angel, and knew the courses of the stars and the powers of herbs, and knew all about the treasures in the earth, and if he knew the qualities of birds and fishes, animals, humans, roots, trees, rocks, and waters, write down and note carefully that true joy is not in that."

And going on a bit farther, St. Francis called again strongly: "Brother Leo, even if a Friar Minor could preach so well that he should convert all infidels to the faith of Christ, write that perfect joy is not there."

Now when he had been talking this way for a distance of two miles, Brother Leo in great amazement asked him: "Father, I beg you in God's name to tell me where perfect joy is."

And St. Francis replied: "When we come to St. Mary of the Angels, soaked by the rain and frozen by the cold, all soiled with mud and suffering from hunger, and we ring at the gate of the Place and the brother porter comes and says angrily: 'Who are you?' And we say: 'We are two of your brothers.' And he contradicts us, saying: 'You are not telling the truth. Rather you are two rascals who go around deceiving people and stealing what they give to the poor. Go away!' And he does not open for us, but makes us stand outside in the snow and rain, cold and hungry, until night falls—then if we endure all those insults and cruel rebuffs patiently, without being troubled and without complaining, and if we reflect humbly and charitably that that porter really knows us and that God makes him speak against us, oh, Brother Leo, write that perfect joy is there!

"And if we continue to knock, and the porter comes out in anger, and drives us away with curses and hard blows like bothersome scoundrels, saying: 'Get away from here, you dirty thieves—go to the hospital! Who do you think you are? You certainly won't eat or sleep here!'—and if we bear it patiently and take the insults with joy and love in our hearts, oh, Brother Leo, write that that is perfect joy!

"And if later, suffering intensely from hunger and the painful cold, with night falling, we still knock and call, and crying loudly beg them to open for us and let us come in for the love of God, and he grows still more angry and says: 'Those fellows are bold and shameless ruffians. I'll give them what they deserve!' And he comes out with a knotty club, and grasping us by the cowl throws us onto the ground, rolling us in the mud and snow, and beats us with that club so much that he covers our bodies with wounds—if we endure all those evils and insults and blows with joy and patience, reflecting that we must accept and bear the sufferings of the Blessed Christ patiently for love of Him, oh, Brother Leo, write that is perfect joy!

"And now hear the conclusion, Brother Leo. Above all the graces and gifts of the Holy Spirit which Christ gives to His friends is that of conquering oneself and willingly enduring sufferings, insults, humiliations, and hardships for the love of Christ. For we cannot glory in all those other marvelous gifts of God, as they are not ours but God's, as the Apostle says: 'What have you that you have not received?'

"But we can glory in the cross of tribulations and afflictions, because that is ours, and so the Apostle says: 'I will not glory save in the Cross of Our Lord Jesus Christ!'"

To whom be honor and glory forever and ever. Amen.[1]

Or simply and plainly, one more story from my own experience.

THE LAST FRENCH FRY

I'm not crazy about fast food, but every once in a while, I do get a "Big Mac attack." So, one Thursday, I went to McDonald's with my oldest friend, Thomas. We've known each other since we were three years old. As usual, I asked him if he wanted to split an order of french fries, and get a large order instead of a small. He said, "No." I was just as happy. I got a large anyway! What's a Big Mac without fries?

When I like what I'm eating, I save parts of what I like till the end. Well, I love the crispy french fries, the tiny ones! So, I always save some for last.

There we were, eating our lunch, and what do you think happened? Just when I'm down to the last crispy fry, guess who now wants one? My friend Thomas!

Can I give it away? Can I let go to make a friend happy? What is my "last french fry" anyway? What can't I, or won't I, give up or let go? What can't you, or won't you, give up or let go? That is the story of and the question of *Kenosis*. Welcome to it!

Notes

Introduction

1. Marion A. Habig, *St. Francis of Assisi, Omnibus of Sources* (Chicago: Franciscan Herald Press, 1973), p. 1448.
2. Henri J.M. Nouwen, *Creative Ministry* (New York: Doubleday & Co., Inc., 1971), p. 110.
3. Joseph Ratzinger, "Is Eucharist a Sacrifice?" *Concilium 24, The Sacraments, An Ecumenical Dilemma*, ed. Hans Kung (New York: Paulist Press, 1966), p. 75.
4. Ibid., p. 73.
5. Eugene C. Kennedy, *Comfort My People: The Pastoral Presence of the Church* (New York: Sheed and Ward, 1968), p. 26.

Chapter One

1. Walter M. Abbot, ed. "Gaudium et Spes," *The Documents of Vatican II* (New York: Guild Press, 1966), p. 263.
2. Jerry Hardy and Mary Streck, *Lent '90* (Bolton, Mass.: Growth Associates, 1990), p. 3.

Chapter Three

1. Richard P. McBrien, *Church: The Continuing Quest* (New York: Newman Press, 1970), p. 73.

Chapter Four

1. Eugene H. Maley, *The Priest and Sacred Scripture* (Washington, D.C.: Publications Office, United States Catholic Conference, 1972), pp. 6-7.
2. Celsus O'Brien, *The Rule of the Friars Minor: A Brief Commentary* (Dublin: Assisi Press, 1954).

3. Ernest E. Larkin and Gerard T. Broccolo, eds., *Spiritual Renewal of the American Priesthood* (Washington, D.C.: Publications Office, United States Catholic Conference, 1972), p. 12.

4. Henri J.M. Nouwen, *The Wounded Healer: Ministry in Contemporary Society* (New York: Doubleday & Co., Inc., 1972), p. 90.

5. Ibid., pp. 93–94.

6. Order of Friars Minor, General Chapter, *The Vocation of the Order Today* (New York: Holy Name Province, Communications Office, 1973), Article 15.

7. Holy Name Province, Provincial Chapter, *Rebuild My House: The Articles of the Extraordinary Chapter of Affairs* (New York: Provincial Communications Office, 1968–69), p. 64.

Epilogue: Perfect Joy of St. Francis

1. Habig, p. 1318.

Select Bibliography

Abbot, Walter M. (ed.). *The Documents of Vatican II*. New York: Guild Press, 1966.

Armstrong, Regis J. and Brady, Ignatius C. *Francis and Clare: The Complete Works*. New York: Paulist Press, 1982.

Brown, Raymond Edward. *Priests and Bishops: Biblical Reflections*. New York: Paulist Press, 1970.

Catholic Biblical Association of America. *The New American Bible*. Paterson, N.J.: St. Anthony Guild Press, 1970.

Evely, Louis. *Suffering*. New York: Herder and Herder, 1967.

Habig, Marion A. *St. Francis of Assisi, Omnibus of Sources*. Franciscan Herald Press, 1973.

Hardy, Jerry and Streck, Mary. *Lent '90*. Bolton, Mass.: Growth Associates, 1990.

Holy Name Province Provincial Chapter. *Rebuild My House: The Articles of the Extraordinary Chapter of Affairs*. New York: Provincial Communication Office, 1969.

Jeremias, Joachim. *New Testament Theology: The Proclamation of Jesus*. New York: Charles Scribner and Sons, 1971.

Kennedy, Eugene C. *Comfort My People: The Pastoral Presence of the Church*. New York: Sheed and Ward, Inc., 1968.

Larkin, Ernest E. and Broccolo, Gerard T. (eds.). *Spiritual Renewal of the American Priesthood*. Washington, D.C.: Publications Office of United States Catholic Conference, 1973.

Maly, Eugene H. *The Priest and Sacred Scripture*. Washington, D.C.: Publications Office of United States Catholic Conference, 1972.

McBrien, Richard P. *Church: The Continuing Quest*. New York: Newman Press, 1970.

Metz, Johannes B. *Poverty of Spirit*. New York: Newman Press, 1968.

———. *Theology of the World*. New York: Herder and Herder, 1969.

Niebuhr, H. Richard. *Christ and Culture*. New York: Harper and Row, 1951.

Nomura, Yushi. *Desert Wisdom: Sayings from the Desert Fathers*. New York: Image Books, Doubleday and Company, 1984.

Nouwen, Henri J.M. *Creative Ministry*. New York: Doubleday and Company, Inc., 1971.

Nouwen, Henri J.M. *The Wounded Healer: Ministry in Contemporary Society*. New York: Doubleday and Company, Inc., 1972.

O'Brien, Celsus. *The Rule of the Friars Minor, A Brief Commentary*. Dublin: Assisi Press, 1954.

Order of Friars Minor, General Chapter. *The Vocation of the Order Today*. New York: Holy Name Province Communications Office, 1973.

Padovano, Anthony T. *Free to be Faithful*. New York: Paulist Press, 1972.

Pittinger, Norman. *Christology Reconsidered*. London: SCM Press, Ltd., 1970.

Ratzinger, Joseph. "Is the Eucharist a Sacrifice?" *Concilium, Vol. XXIV, The Sacraments, an Ecumenical Dilemma*, ed. Hans Kung. New York: Paulist Press, 1966.

Schnackenburg, Rudolf. *Church in the New Testament*. New York: Herder and Herder, 1965.

Stanley, David. *The Apostolic Church in the New Testament*. Westminister, Md.: Newman Press, 1965.

van Kaam, Adrian. *Religion and Personality*. Englewood Cliffs: Prentice-Hall, Inc., 1964.

von Rod, Gerhard. *The Message of the Prophets*. London: SCM Press, 1968.

Zimemrli, W. and Jeremias, J. *Studies in Biblical Theology: The Servant of God*. Naperville, Ill.: Alec. R. Allenson, Inc., 1957.